simply
stations

listening and speaking

• grades k–4 •

For information:

Corwin
A SAGE Company
2455 Teller Road
Thousand Oaks, California 91320
(800) 233-9936
www.corwin.com

SAGE Publications Ltd.
1 Oliver's Yard
55 City Road
London EC1Y 1SP
United Kingdom

SAGE Publications India Pvt. Ltd.
B 1/I 1 Mohan Cooperative
Industrial Area
Mathura Road, New Delhi 110 044
India

SAGE Publications Asia-Pacific Pte. Ltd.
18 Cross Street #10-10/11/12
China Square Central
Singapore 048423

Senior Acquisitions Editor: Tori Bachman

Editorial Development Manager: Julie Nemer

Senior Editorial Assistant: Sharon Wu

Production Editor: Melanie Birdsall

Copy Editor: Heather Kerrigan

Typesetter: Integra

Proofreader: Alison Syring

Cover and Interior Designer: Gail Buschman

Marketing Manager: Deena Meyer

Icon sources: Time-Saving Tip: davooda/Shutterstock.com; EL Tip: iStock.com/ilyaliren

Station icon sources: Listening and Speaking: iStock.com/ilyaliren; Independent Reading: iStock.com/ilyaliren; Partner Reading: iStock.com/ilyaliren; Writing: iStock.com/da-vooda; Poetry: iStock.com/GreenTana; Drama: iStock.com/GreenTana; Word Study: iStock.com/ilyaliren; Inquiry and Research: iStock.com/GreenTana; Let's Talk: iStock.com/ilyaliren; Recording Studio: iStock.com/GreenTana

Library of Congress Cataloging-in-Publication Data

Names: Diller, Debbie, author. | Corwin
Title: Simply stations : listening and speaking, grades K–4 / Debbie Diller.
Other titles: Listening & speaking, grades K–4 | Corwin literacy.
Description: First Edition. | Thousand Oaks, California : Corwin, 2020. | Series: Corwin literacy - CLI; 0
Identifiers: LCCN 2019037644 | ISBN 9781544367163 (Paperback : acid-free paper) | ISBN 9781071802014 (Adobe PDF)
Subjects: LCSH: Language arts (Primary) | Classroom learning centers. | Group work in education. | Education, Primary—Activity programs.
Classification: LCC LB1528 .D55 2020 | DDC 372.6—dc23
LC record available at https://lccn.loc.gov/2019037644

Printed in the United States of America

This book is printed on acid-free paper.

20 21 22 23 24 10 9 8 7 6 5 4 3 2 1

simply
stations

listening and speaking

[
· grades k–4 ·
planning tools
launching lessons
printables
]

resources.corwin.com/simplystations-listening

debbie diller

CORWIN Literacy

Contents

Visit the companion website at
resources.corwin.com/simplystations-listening
for downloadable resources.

iStock.com/monkeybusinessimages

Literacy Stations Overview

Photo by Matthew Rood

The **Listening and Speaking station** is an absolute *must* in a classroom!

Do you have children *learning a new language* in your classroom? You need Listening and Speaking stations! Do you want students to develop *more advanced vocabulary and communication skills*? Include recordings of texts read aloud for children to listen to multiple times and then talk about at a Listening and Speaking station. The Listening and Speaking station can be a powerful place for practice.

You know the value of read alouds for kids—models of fluent, phrased reading, exposure to new vocabulary and concepts, motivation to read those same books and authors, just to name a few. Listening to audiobooks provides extended opportunities for the above and can be a joyful experience for learners of all ages. Listening to a book isn't a substitute for reading; it's an enhancement. As we listen to a text read aloud and then talk about it with a partner, we can focus on comprehension—visualizing, making connections, and thinking deeper about the author's message. And isn't that the ultimate goal of reading?

#simplystations

@debbie.diller
(Instagram)

dillerdebbie
(Facebook)

@debbiediller
(Twitter)

**www.debbiediller
.com** (website)

The Listening and Speaking station is an almost effortless station to introduce at the start of the school year, and it's easy to duplicate so several pairs of students can work at Listening and Speaking stations around your classroom.

In this book, you'll find tons of ideas for simple setup and maintenance, as well as suggestions for adding deeper learning. You'll find everything you need to get started, including what students might listen and respond to, where to get necessary materials and equipment, and how to introduce this station. I've also shared ideas for how to plan with timeless standards, such as describing characters and their interactions, responding to informational text, and using new vocabulary. You'll find ideas for teaching and then transferring these now-familiar skills to the Listening and Speaking station. And a companion website includes all the student-facing tools you'll need in both English and Spanish. My goal is to help you make the Listening and Speaking station a valuable learning experience for students.

This book is dedicated to helping you implement this powerful station in a simple yet meaningful way. I'd love to see and hear your ideas on the Listening and Speaking station, too, so please check in with me on social media using the hashtag #simplystations and share how it's going.

With purposeful practice in mind,
Debbie

Literacy Stations Basics

What Is a Literacy Station?

A literacy station is a small, defined space (stationary or portable) where students **practice** with a **partner**. Students work together on things they **can** do, using **familiar materials** and **tasks** to practice **reading, writing, listening, speaking**, and/or **working with words**. The children use previously taught **academic vocabulary** as they **engage** in **meaningful work** that has been **modeled previously** in whole or small group instruction.

The Listening and Speaking station will likely be portable. Two children will listen to recorded texts read aloud from a device using headphones or earbuds. They will then talk about what they listened to and may write or draw together in response.

How Do Literacy Stations Fit Into the Literacy Block?

In a reading workshop classroom, the literacy block is broken into segments: whole class lessons, small group instruction, and stations work time. Stations work happens simultaneous to small group instruction. As the teacher meets with a small group, the rest of the class works in pairs at **literacy stations** around the classroom. Literacy stations provide purposeful practice.

Around the classroom, pairs of students work together at a variety of stations, including a Listening and Speaking station (or two), a Writing station, two Partner Reading stations, an Independent Reading station, a Word Study station, and a Poetry station. Two children are using retelling pieces and a familiar book at a Drama station; several students are engaged in asking and answering questions at the Inquiry and Research station; and two scholars are talking about a fine art print at the Let's Talk station. (For more information on each station, please see the related title in the Simply Stations series.)

Some stations, such as the Listening and Speaking station, may be duplicated. In the Listening and Speaking station, two students listen to a recorded story on an iPad and then talk about what they read using conversation cards—speech bubbles that guide their discussion. In another Listening and Speaking station, two other children listen to a recorded informational text and jot notes about important ideas they hear. After listening, they talk about their notes and write a response together about what they learned.

EL TIP: Conversation cards will provide sentence stems to help your multilingual students with speaking in response to what they listened to. There are reproducible conversation cards in English and Spanish available on the companion website, **resources.corwin .com/simplystations- listening**.

Each station has been carefully introduced, one at a time, over the first month of school. Students know what is expected of them, they have everything they need, and they are working on tasks they *can* do successfully. In every book of the Simply Stations series, you'll find in-depth suggestions for how to set up and introduce a station.

During the first few weeks of school while children are learning to work at stations, the teacher circulates freely around the classroom facilitating, listening in on students, and talking with them about what they are learning. Once children demonstrate independence with classroom routines for literacy stations (usually about four to six weeks into the school year), the teacher begins to work with small groups. A management board is used to help children move independently to several stations daily. Everything you need for your management board can be found on pages 17–21 of this book!

TIME-SAVING TIP: Set up this station wisely at the start, and it will save you tons of time in the long run. Include all the materials students need, so they don't have to run across the room to grab something. That way they'll "stay" at the "stay-tion"!

What Is the Ideal Number of Students at Each Station?

I recommend having children work in pairs (yes, just two kids!) at each station. This increases student engagement and reduces classroom noise if you space children thoughtfully around the room. You will need more stations, but they will be easier to maintain because you don't have to change things out as often. Use the easy-to-follow directions throughout this series for how to introduce each station to ensure success for you and your students.

How Do I Determine Partnerships?

At the start of the year, think about who gets along well and pair those children together. Once you begin small groups, try pairing students from the same flexible reading group. That way they won't lose their partners when you meet with a group. Also, you'll find that if you plan for things children *can* do, they will push each other further if paired with someone at about the same reading level.

How Long Do Students Work at Each Station?

Each literacy station lasts about twenty minutes in Grades 1–4. In kindergarten, children may spend about fifteen minutes per station. Typically, students go to two rotations back-to-back while the teacher meets with two small groups. If you decide to meet with three groups a day, you might have a whole group lesson after two rounds of stations and then meet with a third small group while all students do independent reading or go to a third round of literacy stations.

How Do Literacy Stations Fit Into the Day?

Literacy stations are just one component in a balanced literacy or a workshop approach to teaching reading and writing. Below are several sample schedules from primary and intermediate classrooms to show where stations fit in the day. Be flexible and create a schedule that works for you.

SAMPLE PRIMARY SCHEDULE for LITERACY

8:00–8:10	Morning Meeting (community building time)
8:10–8:25	Whole Group Lesson for Modeling Using Interactive Read Aloud
8:25–8:45	Literacy Stations and Small Group (round one)
8:45–9:05	Literacy Stations and Small Group (round two)
9:05–9:15	Reflection Time for Stations and Small Group
9:15–9:20	Brain Break
9:20–9:35	Whole Group Lesson for Modeling Using Shared Reading and Word Study
9:35–9:55	Whole Class Independent Reading Time (teacher confers 1:1 or may meet with a third small group)
9:55–10:05	Whole Group Lesson for Modeling Writing
10:05–10:30	Whole Class Independent Writing Time (teacher confers with students 1:1 or may meet with a small group for writing)
10:30–10:40	Reflection Time for Writing

SAMPLE INTERMEDIATE SCHEDULE for LITERACY

8:00–8:10	Morning Meeting (community building time; students do book talks/share what they're reading)
8:10–8:30	Whole Group Lesson for Modeling Using Interactive Read Aloud or Shared Reading Integrating Word Study/Vocabulary
8:30–8:50	Whole Class Independent Reading Time (teacher confers 1:1 or may meet with a small group for reading)
8:50–9:00	Literacy Stations, Book Clubs, and Small Group (some teachers do another twenty-minute round of stations if schedules allow)
9:00–9:15	Whole Group Lesson for Modeling Writing
9:15–9:40	Whole Class Independent Writing Time (teacher confers with students 1:1 or may meet with a small group for writing)
9:40–9:50	Reflection Time for Reading and Writing

How Long Is It Going to Take Me to Prepare for These Stations?

I've included time-saving tips in each book to help ease preparation. The most important thing to remember is to take what you're teaching and *transfer those materials and tasks* to each literacy station. Don't make (or buy) a bunch of stuff just for stations!

How Often Should the Teacher Change Things at a Station?

Stations are not changed out weekly but involve **spiral reviews** with young scholars returning to work multiple times over several weeks with the same materials and tasks. It's okay for children to listen to recorded books more than once at the Listening and Speaking station, especially if it's a favorite text. **Spiral review** means that students keep practicing things multiple times throughout the year.

For example, if you've been teaching children about characters and their traits and relationships, students can keep practicing this all year long at the Listening and Speaking station, and then also at the Partner Reading station. You don't need to have kids do this only the week you've taught it. When students become familiar with characters and character traits, it will be easier for them to transfer what they're learning to new books in a series or to new characters with similar traits.

In Section 3 of this book, I'll show you how to teach and then have children practice for transfer in the Listening and Speaking station using what you've already taught. (No need to constantly create or purchase new station materials!)

Simply change out **what** students listen to and how they **respond** over time. Be intentional with your changes. Pay attention to student interests and how their understanding is deepening. Ask for children's input when possible.

Why Are Literacy Stations Effective?

- This is **meaningful** work for the rest of the class during small group time.

- Children like to **talk** and to work with their **peers**. Enjoyment increases engagement!

- **Partner practice** helps students become **independent of the teacher**. Kids aren't working alone. They practice *with* a partner, doing tasks together.

- **Choice** and **student ownership** promote independence. At the Listening and Speaking station, students should have a choice of several recordings to listen to. They may also make recordings for others to listen to, which promotes student ownership.

- **Transfer of learning** occurs as scholars work with familiar tasks and materials previously modeled by the teacher. For example, at the Listening and Speaking station, partners respond to recorded text using graphic organizers and academic vocabulary taught during whole group instruction.

- **English Learners (EL)** and children with language-based learning differences especially benefit from additional time to work at the Listening and Speaking station. They need opportunities to listen to learn language. Look for EL Tips throughout this book.

Pairs of students work in well-defined small spaces around the classroom during stations time. Two kids use laptops as a Listening and Speaking station at desks against the wall.

The Listening and Speaking station is duplicated in this classroom. Each Listening and Speaking station is numbered and placed on either side of a cabinet to create defined, separate spaces and minimize distractions. Students listen to different texts at each station.

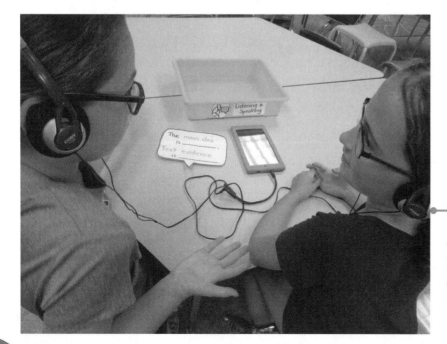

Partners use a conversation card to practice familiar academic vocabulary after listening to informational text on a tablet at this nonfiction Listening and Speaking station.

Getting Started
With Stations

Do you feel overwhelmed about all your students working with partners around the room? Creating a plan for setting up stations and introducing them to your class, one station at a time, will help both you and your students experience success.

Plan for Physical Space

1 Make a list of stations you'd like to have in your classroom. Begin with the end in mind. If you list stations you might want to have for the year, it will help you when planning for space.

You'll want to include some stationary stations and others that are portable to utilize every inch of space in your classroom. I've included a sample list below and space for you to make your own list. You might label stationary stations with an "S" and portable ones with a "P," as shown. Remember that you can duplicate a station, too! You'll want enough for everyone to partner up. And, yes, if you have twenty-two kids, plan for eleven small spaces around the room. (Don't worry—I'll show you how to introduce each station, one at a time!)

SAMPLE LIST of LITERACY STATIONS	LITERACY STATIONS I PLAN to SET UP
• Listening and Speaking station – P • Independent Reading station – S/P • Partner Reading station – S/P • Writing station – S • Poetry station – S • Drama station – P • Word Study station – S/P • Let's Talk station – P • Inquiry and Research station – S	

2 Create a classroom map of your space with a colleague using chart paper and sticky notes. If you work together, you can help each other decide if there are things in your space that could move or be eliminated. And you may be able to use similar designs in neighboring classrooms!

a. Draw in permanent fixtures like windows, doors, closets, technology, etc. on the perimeter of your paper. (Don't draw desks or tables yet. Save them until the end.)

b. Using sticky notes, plan for where to place your whole group and small group teaching areas. Don't put them on top of each other! Balance these big spaces. Make a sticky note for your classroom library, too, and use this space as a focal point. This will become your Independent Reading station during stations time and a place for students to choose books for other independent reading times.

c. Using additional sticky notes, label each with a station you'd like to have. Use the list you created in step 1. Think about which may be portable, like the Listening and Speaking station, and which may be stationary, like the Poetry station (with a pocket chart attached to a wall or bulletin board). Place these sticky notes around the perimeter first and then fill in interior spaces. To minimize noise and distractions, decide how to space out your stations so they aren't on top of each other.

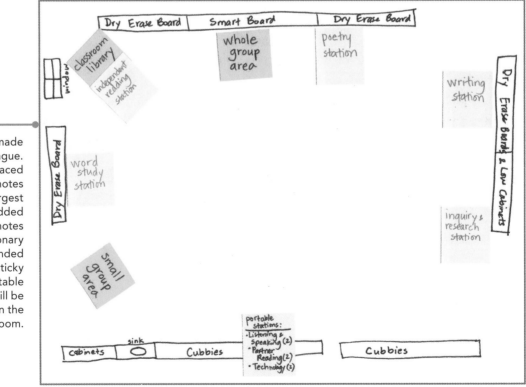

Classroom map made with a colleague. First, we placed yellow sticky notes to show the largest areas. Then we added pink sticky notes to show stationary stations. We ended with a blue sticky note listing portable stations that will be taken to desks in the middle of the room.

d. Move around sticky notes until you have a workable plan, keeping flexibility in mind. Be open to changing things if the flow doesn't work.

e. Work with your colleague to place furniture in your classroom using your map. Place desks and tables *last, not first*. They will fit! It's like a puzzle. Place the perimeter pieces first and then fill in the middle of your classroom.

f. Don't try to make every piece of furniture fit if it doesn't work. Most classrooms have more "stuff" than is needed. Be sure to leave space for children.

MY CLASSROOM MAP

Make a Stations Roll-Out Plan

3 Plan to introduce one station at a time. Think about what your students need to practice and what they *can* do early in the year. Start slowly and simply. Which will you introduce first, second, and so on?

I have found over the years that introducing Independent Reading, followed by Partner Reading and then Listening and Speaking, offers the smoothest modeling, learning, and practicing. Then introduce additional stations according to your students' needs and your curriculum and standards.

OUR BEGINNING-of-the-YEAR STATIONS
1. Independent Reading station
2. Partner Reading station
3. Listening and Speaking station

OUR BEGINNING-of-the-YEAR STATIONS
1. _____
2. _____
3. _____

See Section 2 of each book in the Simply Stations series for Launch Lessons for each specific station. You'll also find an accompanying Checklist of Routines to Model and Expect for the station.

Model and explain your expectations. Then have all students try the station in your whole group area, so you can monitor and assist. Do this for several days with one station until you're sure students will be able to do this independently of you.

4 Once your students seem to be doing the first station independently, introduce the next station. Follow step 2 again for this station.

Introduce independent reading routines to the whole class at their seats.

On another day, introduce partner reading routines to the whole class around the carpet perimeter.

5 When students are showing independence with these two routines (which will become the Independent Reading station and the Partner Reading station), try assigning half the class to the first station and the other half to the new one.

In a few days, have half the class do Independent Reading while the other half works at a Partner Reading station.

6 Continue to layer on one station at a time, in this way, until you have enough stations for students to work in pairs. There is no perfect number of stations. Do what works best for your children and you. When your students know how to do three or four stations well, introduce the management board.

See pages 17–21 in this section for how to create and introduce a management board.

7 Once students can use the management board to work in their stations independently of you, layer on meeting with small groups. The foundational process leading to this step usually takes about four to six weeks in most classrooms. Add the Meet With Teacher icon to your management board.

Again, see page 17 of this section on Literacy Stations Management Board How-To.

Start small group teaching when students can work independently of you.

8 Add new stations, one at a time, as you teach with new standards and change out materials as students show you they are ready.

Use the planning tool and roll-out calendar found on the companion website, **resources.corwin.com/simplystations-listening**, to help you plan for when and how you might introduce each new station.

Take your time introducing each station thoughtfully. Be sure students understand your expectations and *can* do what you want them to do at that station before moving on to the next one. Your investment in time will pay off.

Are There Special Considerations for Kindergarten Roll-Out?

In kindergarten, follow the above plan but start the first week of school with placeholders for stations. Think about what your children can do independent of the teacher at their tables and introduce one activity for each table group. Possibilities include partner playdough, partner puzzles, tracing, reading easy books from a basket on the table by talking about the pictures, or drawing pictures on plain white paper with colored pencils.

Sample Planning Calendar (K–1)
for Stations Roll-Out and Refresh

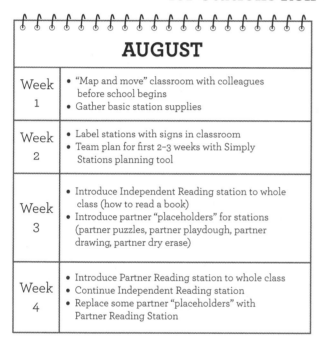

AUGUST

Week 1	• "Map and move" classroom with colleagues before school begins • Gather basic station supplies
Week 2	• Label stations with signs in classroom • Team plan for first 2–3 weeks with Simply Stations planning tool
Week 3	• Introduce Independent Reading station to whole class (how to read a book) • Introduce partner "placeholders" for stations (partner puzzles, partner playdough, partner drawing, partner dry erase)
Week 4	• Introduce Partner Reading station to whole class • Continue Independent Reading station • Replace some partner "placeholders" with Partner Reading Station

SEPTEMBER

Week 1	• Introduce Listening and Speaking station • Use checklist for operating listening before sending kids there • Introduce Word Study station using kids' names • Replace some partner "placeholders"
Week 2	• Introduce Poetry station with familiar nursery rhymes and poems • Replace some partner "placeholders" • Introduce the management board
Week 3	• Introduce Writing station with lists and bucket fillers • Introduce Let's Talk station with describing photos • Replace some partner "placeholders" • Refresh Independent Reading and Partner Reading stations
Week 4	• Introduce Drama station • Refresh Listening and Speaking and Word Study stations

OCTOBER

Week 1	• Refresh Poetry and Writing stations • Introduce Inquiry and Research station
Week 2	• Refresh Let's Talk and Drama stations
Week 3	• Refresh Independent Reading and Partner Reading stations
Week 4	• Refresh Listening and Speaking and Word Study stations

NOVEMBER

Week 1	• Refresh Poetry and Writing stations
Week 2	• Refresh Let's Talk and Drama stations
Week 3	
Week 4	• Refresh Inquiry and Research station

DECEMBER

Week 1	• Refresh Independent Reading and Partner Reading stations
Week 2	• Refresh Listening and Speaking and Word Study stations
Week 3	
Week 4	

(Continued)

(Continued)

JANUARY

Week 1	• Refresh Poetry and Writing stations
Week 2	• Refresh Let's Talk and Drama stations
Week 3	• Refresh Inquiry and Research station
Week 4	• Refresh Independent Reading and Partner Reading stations

FEBRUARY

Week 1	• Refresh Listening and Speaking and Word Study stations
Week 2	• Refresh Poetry and Writing stations
Week 3	• Refresh Let's Talk and Drama stations
Week 4	• Refresh Inquiry and Research station

MARCH

Week 1	• Refresh Independent Reading and Partner Reading stations
Week 2	• Refresh Listening and Speaking and Word Study stations
Week 3	• Refresh Poetry and Writing stations
Week 4	• Refresh Let's Talk and Drama stations

APRIL

Week 1	• Refresh Inquiry and Research station
Week 2	• Refresh Independent Reading and Partner Reading stations
Week 3	• Refresh Listening and Speaking and Word Study stations
Week 4	• Refresh Poetry and Writing stations

MAY

Week 1	• Refresh Let's Talk and Drama stations
Week 2	• Refresh Inquiry and Research station
Week 3	• Refresh stations as needed
Week 4	• Refresh stations as needed • Reflect and make notes for next year

NOTES

Rotate the table group placeholder activities for the first week or two of school while you begin teaching things that can move into literacy stations. For example, as you read books aloud, place them in the classroom library and Independent Reading station. During read aloud, teach kindergartners to think and talk about characters. When you introduce the Listening and Speaking station, students will be ready to listen for characters and talk about them.

Starting the second or third week of school, replace placeholders with literacy stations, one at a time, until you have phased out table group activities. Within the first month or so, you should have several literacy stations up and running. Small group instruction should start between the sixth and eighth week of kindergarten.

Literacy Stations Management Board How-To

After you've established several literacy stations in your classroom, you can help children work independently by setting up a management board. The management board will save time by showing kids where to go throughout stations time without you having to direct them every step of the way. Once children know how to read the management board and understand what to do at stations, you can simply dismiss them (several at a time) to their first station.

Setting Up the Management Board

Feel free to adjust any of the following ideas to create a system that works for you and your students. For instance, many teachers I've worked with over the years prefer a simple management board made with a pocket chart. Another idea is to put magnetic tape on the back of cards and place them on a magnetic white board. Or, you can project a management board on a screen using a PowerPoint template. You can even embed a digital timer in it! No matter how you present the management board, the basic structure will remain the same. In the end, the goal is for students to be able to refer to it independently during stations time.

The directions that follow are for creating a traditional management board with a pocket chart in a self-contained classroom.

> **TIME-SAVING TIP:** Take a photo of each student during the first week of school. These photos can be used on your management board (electronic or print), but can also be used at several stations, including the Writing station (students can practice writing their names and those of classmates) and the Word Study station (students can sort names in the lower grades and put them in ABC order in the upper grades).

iStock.com

In a first-grade classroom, the teacher uses photos of the students and their accompanying stations icons on a pocket chart. She uses Meet With Teacher cards to show which students she will meet with during small group instruction today while the rest of the class is at literacy stations.

1 Start by taking a photo of each of your students and/or write their names on individual cards that fit in a pocket chart. A 3-x-5 size name card usually works well.

2 Make icon cards to match each station you'll have. You can find icon printables at **resources.corwin.com/simplystations-listening**, or you can take photos of each station to use as an icon instead. You'll need two copies of each icon, one for the first rotation and another for the second rotation. (If you decide to have three rotations, make three copies of each icon.) And, if you duplicate stations, you may want to number the extras (e.g., Word Study station 1, Word Study station 2, and so on).

3 Pair students using photos/name cards on the left side of the pocket chart. (This is important, because we want kids to read from left to right.) If you have an odd number of students, you could have one group of three, or a child could work alone.

4 To keep children from losing their partners during small group, consider pairing children who are in the same flexible reading group. You'll find that students working on the same level push each other forward.

5 Place two icon cards beside each pair of students to show which stations they'll go to each day. (These show where students go for the first rotation, then the second rotation.) If you have students go to three rotations, place three icon cards beside each pair of students.

6 Print Meet With Teacher cards for each pair of students you meet with in small group for that rotation. (For example, if you're meeting with four students in small group, you'll need two Meet With Teacher cards.) Place the Meet With Teacher cards over an icon card in the first or second rotation, depending on when you'll meet a group.

Now the management board is ready for kids to read when they enter your room. Teach them to read it on their own so they can quickly and easily go to stations during literacy stations time.

Daily Use of the Management Board

a. At the start of stations/small group time, dismiss several students at a time to go to their first station. Having only a few kids moving at once simplifies classroom management and prevents a chaotic start to stations time. You want children to move calmly and quietly to their station and get started right away. Playing calm background music during stations time may help.

b. Use an audible signal (bell, chime, music) when it's time to switch to the next rotation. This may take some practice, but kids usually get the hang of it within a few days. Some teachers use an online timer with a built-in message that it's time to switch.

c. At the end of each day, simply remove your Meet With Teacher cards and place them to the side. Rotate literacy stations icons down to the next space on the board. Then place tomorrow's Meet With Teacher cards over the top of stations icons beside the children you'll meet with next in the first or second small group rotation.

d. Finally, look over the board to be sure children will be practicing at stations where they'll get the most benefit. You may decide to move a station icon to match what a particular pair of students needs most. For example, if you notice that two students are scheduled to go to the Independent Reading station but they really need more time to listen to stories, move the Listening and Speaking station icon beside their names and move the Independent Reading icon to another spot for children who need more opportunities to read independently.

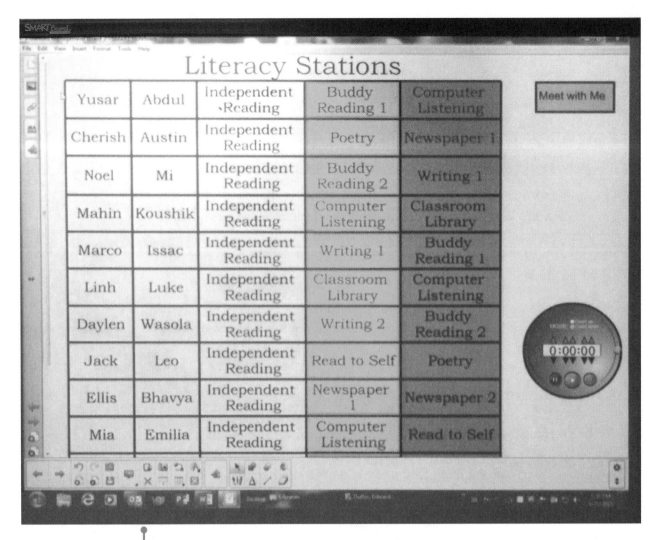

Literacy Stations

Yusar	Abdul	Independent Reading	Buddy Reading 1	Computer Listening
Cherish	Austin	Independent Reading	Poetry	Newspaper 1
Noel	Mi	Independent Reading	Buddy Reading 2	Writing 1
Mahin	Koushik	Independent Reading	Computer Listening	Classroom Library
Marco	Issac	Independent Reading	Writing 1	Buddy Reading 1
Linh	Luke	Independent Reading	Classroom Library	Computer Listening
Daylen	Wasola	Independent Reading	Writing 2	Buddy Reading 2
Jack	Leo	Independent Reading	Read to Self	Poetry
Ellis	Bhavya	Independent Reading	Newspaper 1	Newspaper 2
Mia	Emilia	Independent Reading	Computer Listening	Read to Self

Meet with Me

0:00:00

You might use a PowerPoint for your management board, projected for the class to see during stations. Integrate a timer if you'd like, too.

This upper-grade teacher used a small space on a dry-erase magnetic white board for her management board. She used photos of each station as icons and wrote the names of stations and who would go there under the station.

Jada	Miguel	Partner Reading Station	Writing Station	Logan	Makayla
Ava	Xavier	Meet With Teacher	Poetry Station	Noah	Alyssa
Gabriella	Jordan	Meet With Teacher	Drama Station	Maverick	Destiny
Amelia	Jayden	Independent Reading Station	Partner Reading Station	Josh	Emma
Genevieve	Gabriel	Independent Reading Station	Listening and Speaking Station	Zach	Martina

Portion of the management board in a departmentalized upper-grade classroom.

Class 1 is pictured on the left with green cards.

Class 2 is on the right with pink cards.

Move the icons (not the names) down a space daily.

Meet With Teacher icons are inserted as needed.

Listening and Speaking Station Basics

Why Include This Station?

Listening and speaking lead to learning language.

Daily partner practice in a Listening and Speaking station is important because listening to and talking about audiobooks

- Is fun for learners of all ages, especially if students get to choose what they listen to

- Provides models of phrased, fluent reading with dramatic voices

- Gives students opportunities to "read" text at higher reading levels

- Helps kids use some of the same vocabulary used in the text

- Exposes students to new genres they might not have read on their own

EL TIP: Read aloud is a perfect opportunity for children to hear language, but there aren't enough hours in the day for the teacher to read aloud to students over and over again. So, the Listening and Speaking station can be a crucial, repeated read aloud opportunity for children who are learning English as a new language.

Young children learn language by listening. Babies listen for a year or more before they begin using words and eventually sentences. We consume (or hear) new vocabulary before we begin producing (or speaking and writing) those same words. In much the same way, listening comprehension precedes reading comprehension. If children have trouble identifying characters, settings, and plots when they *listen* to stories, it will be even more difficult for them to comprehend these story elements when reading on their own.

Combine listening with speaking, and you have a winning combination! As students listen and then talk with a partner about characters, settings, and plots, they will practice using language purposefully. Instead of having kids listen and then fill in worksheets, having them discuss what they read can deepen comprehension and build vocabulary. Use the lessons in Section 3 of this book to teach students exactly how to do this. With these new tools, you will probably want to have a Listening and Speaking station set up all year long!

The Listening and Speaking station is one of the easiest to establish early in the school year. All you need is something for learners to listen to and equipment for them to listen with. Find a comfortable place for children to sit for the Listening and Speaking station. Some teachers use pillows on the floor or a low, small table to define this space. Others have students take the materials to a student desk if space is limited. Some teachers use recordings on iPads or tablets; others use CD players or laptops. You can use commercially produced recordings, or simply read books into a microphone yourself. There are many possibilities for obtaining materials for kids to listen to. See Section 4 for resource ideas.

The main thing children do at this station is listen to recordings, so you'll want to provide a variety of materials for them to listen to: nonfiction books, news articles, poems, music, and stories. Set a purpose for listening and speaking to increase the benefits at this station; you'll see more about this idea in Section 3 when we lean in to teaching for transfer. Add oral response over time, as you teach children *how to* respond to literature and informational text. Writing may also be added later in the year, but only if it deepens student understanding (and you've modeled it well). Remember, the Listening and Speaking station connects to concepts you've taught or are teaching to the whole group based on your curriculum, standards, and students' needs. (Again, Section 3 of this book digs deeper into planning for, teaching, and rolling out stations with clear intent.)

When considering what books or materials to include in the Listening and Speaking station, think about your purposes for listening and the needs of the children who are working there. You might provide books a grade level above student independent reading level to expose them to higher-level text and new vocabulary. Or, you might have students listen to books on their instructional reading level to provide models for fluent reading that they can replicate as they read the books on their own right afterward. Also consider the interests of your kids when choosing books for the Listening and Speaking station. This will increase student engagement and may encourage them to read these same books on their own. Search for texts that reflect the cultural background of your class to help them make connections that may deepen comprehension and increase reading motivation.

TIME-SAVING TIP: This station shouldn't take a lot of time to prepare. You might plan to set aside a regular time every two weeks to download and plan. Use the roll-out calendar at **resources.corwin.com/simplystations-listening** to help you think about this ahead of time. Work with your grade-level team to divide and conquer. Ask each team member to find three to five recorded titles that correspond with what you're teaching when it's his/her turn. Rotate this job. If there are four teachers on your team, you'll only have to do this every eight weeks or so!

What Do Students Do *at* This Station?

Partners work together to practice listening and responding to recorded text using graphic organizers and academic vocabulary introduced during whole group instruction.

Here's what you should see at the Listening and Speaking station:

- Two students sit beside each other in a small space sharing one listening device and two sets of headphones hooked into a splitter, so both children can listen to the same text together.

- A copy of the book may be included, so they can read along.

- Listening and Speaking stations can be portable, so they can be used in a small space such as a student desk or on the floor.

- This station can be duplicated, so multiple pairs of children are listening and speaking to a variety of texts around the classroom. Some classrooms have separate nonfiction and fiction Listening and Speaking stations. (A variety of other stations are in use during this time, too! See other books in the Simply Stations series for ideas.)

- Devices like tablets and laptops simplify operating a Listening and Speaking station, but good old tape recorders and CD players work, too.

A pair of students listen to a recorded book and follow along.

Children view and listen to a recorded story. Then they use the book to retell what they heard.

Here is a sampling of the types of work students may do at a Listening and Speaking station with a partner. (Ideas on how to develop this work are found in Section 3 of this book.) Pairs of students may be

- Listening to a recorded text or audiobook (fiction, poetry, informational text, podcast) using a splitter to share a device

- Talking about what they listened to (using conversation cards to prompt specific talk), such as:

  ○ characters and their interactions

  ○ settings and their importance to a plot

  ○ plots, conflicts, and resolutions in stories

  ○ words authors used to create imagery

  ○ new information learned about a topic

  ○ asking and answering questions about what they heard

- Using graphic organizers to jot down specifics connected to what they listened to

- Using new vocabulary to talk about what they listened to

- Taking notes/drawing pictures about information they heard

- Following directions to make something

- Recording and listening to their own reading

To utilize a Listening and Speaking station effectively in your classroom, it's helpful to brainstorm with your students what they might do here. I like to create an I Can list, such as the samples pictured below, to clarify expectations for this station. The I Can list helps students work independently in the station, and it reminds them of learning expectations; they'll start to see the connections between your instruction and what they do in stations.

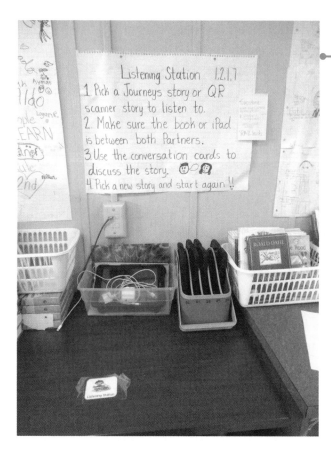

Here is a sample I Can list made with a second-grade class.

EL TIP: Include photos or simple sketches on your I Can lists so multilingual children can easily read these.

TIME-SAVING TIP: Ask students for ideas of what they'd like to listen to at this station, too. Learners in Grades 3–4 might help find books for others to listen to. A responsible student (or two) might have the classroom job of Recorded Book Selector.

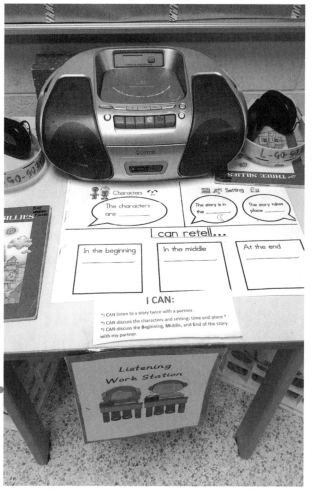

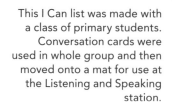

This I Can list was made with a class of primary students. Conversation cards were used in whole group and then moved onto a mat for use at the Listening and Speaking station.

How Do I Keep This Station Varied *and* Fresh?

To keep the Listening and Speaking station fresh and working well throughout the year, try the suggestions listed below.

- Use QR codes to help students easily locate recordings online to listen to. You might ask your school librarian to make a page with a photo of a book, the matching QR code, and a summary of the book. Place this in a clear plastic sleeve at the Listening and Speaking station to help students choose books to listen to.

- Duplicate this station to have a *fiction* Listening and Speaking station and a separate *nonfiction* Listening and Speaking station.

- If you teach in a dual language classroom, have an English Listening and Speaking station *and* a Spanish (or Mandarin or Arabic) Listening and Speaking station. Provide audiobooks recorded in each language for children to listen to at a station with the matching language labeled there.

- Over time, you might change the Listening and Speaking station to a recording studio. Simply use an iPad and a book. Students read and video/record themselves. Afterward, they can play it back and listen to how they sound while using a fluency reflection tool. (A printable tool is available on the companion website, **resources.corwin.com/simplystations-listening**.)

- Have students make recordings for other classrooms and/or grade levels. This is a great way to give struggling readers in upper grades a purpose for practicing reading lower-level books aloud. You might include a photo and name of the reader to personalize this.

EL TIP: Invite adults and older students who speak the home language of your multilingual students to create recorded books in your language of instruction for students to listen to. They may have different accents than the voice actors who make commercial audiobooks, and this may help your students connect.

- Make your own recordings for the Listening and Speaking station by recording a favorite read aloud. Invite parents, other teachers, and administrators to make recordings for the Listening and Speaking station, too. Again, adding a photo of the reader adds an element of fun.

- In upper grades, integrate social studies into the Listening and Speaking station by having students listen to speeches by great orators. The website www.learnoutloud.com has a nice compilation of recorded speeches. TED talks (https://www.ted.com/playlists/86/talks_to_watch_with_kids) are a great resource for this as well. You might add a printed copy of the speech, too, so students can follow along. To improve comprehension, teach scholars how to take notes or pay attention to new vocabulary as they listen. They might also practice reading parts of a speech and recording it to practice oratory skills.

- In a classroom with hearing-impaired students, you might use assistive listening devices. Check with an audiologist for the best way to help students listen to recorded books.

- Pair books (in print or braille) with audio supported learning for blind or visually impaired students to build listening skills, too.

TIME-SAVING TIP: Ask your media specialist (at school or a local public library) to help you find recordings and possibly create related QR codes appropriate for your students' reading levels.

This student uses a QR code to locate a recording at the Listening and Speaking station.

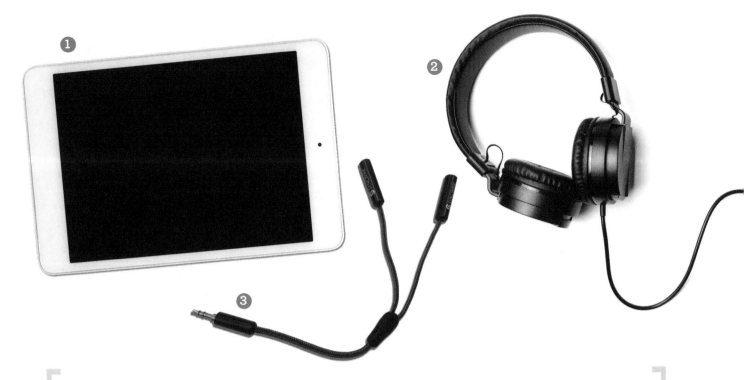

What Are *the* Essential Materials?

Listening and Speaking stations require a combination of low- and high-tech tools. Use what you have at your school. Some materials you'll want to help you get started setting up a Listening and Speaking station are included here.

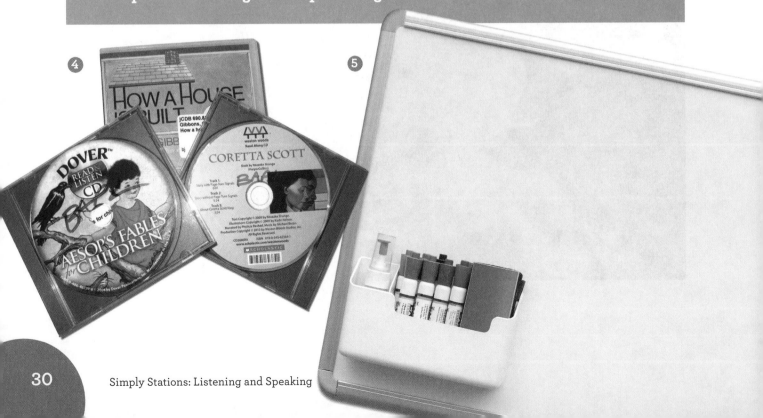

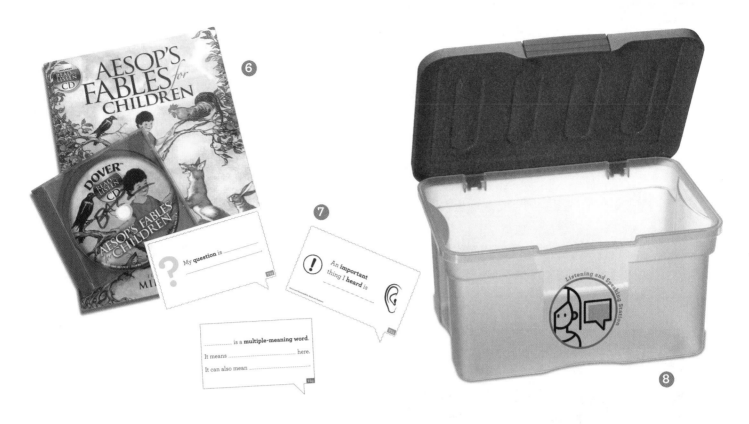

① Technology for playing back audiobooks (e.g., tablet, CD player, laptop)

② Headphones or earbuds

③ Splitter (so two students can listen to one device)

④ Recorded books or articles in a format compatible with your technology

⑤ Dry erase supplies for response

⑥ Print books or articles that correspond to the recordings (just one copy for two students to share)

⑦ Conversation cards to support oral response (speaking)

⑧ Basket to hold listening supplies

⑨ Graphic organizers for response

⑩ Place for two kids to sit

How Do I Set Up This Station?

You don't need a lot of space for the Listening and Speaking station. And remember, you might have several of these! They can be portable and carried to a desk or table. Or they can be stationary and set up in one permanent spot.

This Listening and Speaking station utilizes Command hooks that hold headphones low on a wall where children can easily access materials.

The end of a built-in island becomes a stationary Listening and Speaking station with everything kids need at their fingertips.

Older students simply sit on the floor at this space-saving Listening and Speaking station.

This classroom has furniture that comfortably houses a compact Listening and Speaking station in a small space.

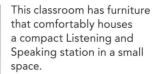

You might utilize a computer as a Listening and Speaking station, too. These students are listening to Tumblebooks.

How Do I Introduce *the* Listening *and* Speaking Station?

It's vital that you model what you expect at a station, so that children know exactly what to do and how to do it. Model, model, model! And don't be afraid to stop and reteach if students aren't using materials correctly. Here are some step-by-step procedures to help you introduce the Listening and Speaking station. (Also see the Launch Lesson on page 37 for introducing this station.)

1. One of the most important things you'll want to do to get started with Listening and Speaking stations is to show students how to use the equipment and technology. If you're using an iPad or tablet, model how to find the appropriate pieces to listen to. For example, teach children how to scan a QR code to get to the online recorded book quickly and easily. If you're using a CD player, teach students how to insert the CD properly and how to operate the device (color-code buttons with a green dot for start and a red dot for stop).

You might make a chart like this to clarify expectations at the Listening and Speaking station.

Do's and Don'ts at Listening & Speaking

DO:	DON'T:
1. BEFORE LISTENING... -Find what you'll listen to quickly with your partner. -Plug in the splitter and headsets or earbuds tightly.	-Don't look for games to play. -Don't argue about what to listen to.
2. DURING LISTENING... -Follow along as you listen. -Take your headsets or earbuds off if you talk with your partner.	-Don't push PLAY until your partner is ready. -Don't talk to your partner unless you push PAUSE and remove your headset or earbuds.
3. AFTER LISTENING... -Talk with your partner about what you listened to. -Put the iPad in the basket when done. -Put your headsets or earbuds away carefully.	-Don't get off topic or talk loudly with your partner. -Don't stand on the iPad when it's cleanup time.

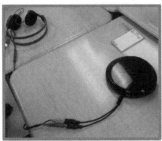

Before Listening

During Listening

After Listening

Draw picture directions with your class, if needed. You might review and post a Dos and Don'ts chart for how to use the equipment at the Listening and Speaking station.

Colored dots help students know exactly how to operate equipment at this Listening and Speaking station.

2. Demonstrate how to work with headsets/earbuds, as well as how to use the splitter so partners can listen to a recording on one device. Model how to gently push the jack in until there is a good connection. (If this is a portable station, show how to take the headsets/earbuds out of the container gently *and* put them away carefully.) You might take a photo of students using this station and post it as a model of how to wear headsets with a splitter attached.

3. Have students take turns trying out the listening technology with a partner to demonstrate that they understand operation and procedures before opening the Listening and Speaking station. Use a checklist (available on the companion website, **resources.corwin .com/simplystations-listening**) to show when kids have passed the "operating test." Then allow them to use this station.

4. Model how to stop the recording and remove their headsets/earbuds when students want to talk with their partner about what they're listening to.

5. Show students how to share a book by having each child hold one side of the book while listening to the recording.

6. Model cleanup thoroughly. Show how to put away the headsets or earbuds, so they are ready for the next use. (Some teachers have children bring their own earbuds as a school supply and store each set in an individual snack-size zip top bag labeled with the child's name. Place these in one basket for boys and another for girls to make them easier for students to access.) Model how to put the iPad or small CD player in a basket before standing up and putting this away. (If kids are sitting on the floor, be sure they put the iPad in a basket *before* standing up so they don't crack the iPad screen.)

7. In whole group lessons using read aloud, model how to respond to books with a partner. Over time, move these same responding options to the Listening and Speaking station for students to practice when talking about texts with a partner. (See Section 3: Planning and Teaching for ideas.)

Photo by Matthew Rood

LAUNCH LESSON for the LISTENING and SPEAKING STATION

Here is a sample lesson to use for introducing the Listening and Speaking station. Teaching routines well will minimize interruptions over time. Teach this lesson as often as needed. Students may need to be reminded of your expectations for their behavior at this station, so be as explicit as possible.

Have all equipment at your fingertips as you model. Place materials for the Listening and Speaking station in a small basket labeled with the name of this station. Also have the space labeled in the classroom where students will use this station. (You might enlarge the Listening and Speaking icon or use the printable sign found on the companion website, **resources .corwin.com/simplystations-listening**.)

You can break this lesson into several parts, depending on the age and experience of students in your classroom.

INTRODUCING THE SPACE

- Gather students in your whole group teaching space. Ask them to read the label on the basket and point to the matching sign in the classroom. Have a student model as your "partner" at this station.

- Set the purpose for this station, and model how to use the materials here. Say: *At the Listening and Speaking station, you and your partner will work together to listen and respond to recorded books. Listening and speaking about what you've heard will help you learn new words and information and enjoy stories. Everything you need is in this labeled basket. When it's your turn to go to this station, take the basket to the space that matches it.* (You might have several pairs of students take turns modeling what this will look like.)

INTRODUCING THE LISTENING EQUIPMENT

- Demonstrate how to work with headsets/earbuds, as well as how to use the splitter so partners can listen to a recording on one device. Model how to gently push the jack in until there is a good connection.

  - Say: *Take out the headsets and splitter and plug them in like this. Work quietly so you don't disturb students at other stations.* (You might take a photo of students using this station and post it as a model of how to wear headsets with a splitter attached.)

- Model how to start and stop the equipment.

  - Say: *This is the on button. This is the off button. Here is the pause button to push if you want to stop and talk to your partner about what you heard.*

- Show students how to quickly find the appropriate pieces to listen to.

  - Say: *It's important to spend your time listening and speaking, not looking for a book!*

  - If you're using an iPad or tablet, model how to find the appropriate pieces to listen to. Say: *This is how to scan a QR code to get to the online recorded book quickly. Or say: Click on this icon to take you to the page I have marked. Decide what to listen to with your partner.*

  - If you're using a CD player, say: *This is how to insert the CD into the player. Then push the green dot to start. Push the red dot to stop. Hold the matching book with your partner and follow along as you listen.*

- Draw picture directions with your class, if needed, on a chart for easy reference.

- Before listening, remind students to be sure they can hear.

  - Say: *To get a good connection, gently push the jack into the port until it is tight. Do a sound check to be sure you can both hear. If you can't hear, what can you do?*

- Problem solve before problems arise to minimize interruptions later! Model how to use volume controls and check for connectivity. You might have a Tech Expert as a classroom job. Have students ask this student for help rather than interrupting you.

INTRODUCING RESPONSE

- Demonstrate for students how to speak about what they listened to.

  - Say: *After you've listened to the recording, talk about what you heard. Be sure to stop the recording and remove your headsets when you talk to each other.* (Stop and show them how to do this.)

- Then give learners guidelines for response.

  - Say: *Sometimes I will put conversation cards like this in the basket to remind you of what you might talk about. Other times there may be paper to use for taking notes or drawing pictures about what you heard. Today, we will use the card that we're using in whole group.*

- ○ Show students how to respond. For example, if you have a card that says *The main character in this story is _____. This character _____.* Model how to read the card together and talk about that character (name, feelings, actions, and why). Then you might show how to work with a partner to draw a picture of that character with a speech bubble showing what the character would say (for younger students) or make a character map (for older students). (See lessons in Timeless Standard 1 in Section 3 for specifics.)

INTRODUCING CLEAN UP

- ● Model how to return materials to the container carefully and quietly when it is time to clean up.

  - ○ Say: *When I give the cleanup signal, put things away quietly and carefully. Unplug the headsets and splitter. Put the materials back neatly in the container, like this. That will make it easy for the next kids to use the Listening and Speaking station.*

TRYING IT OUT

- ● Have students take turns trying out the listening technology with a partner to demonstrate that they understand operation and procedures before opening the Listening and Speaking station. Use a checklist (available on the companion website, **resources.corwin .com/simplystations-listening**) to show when kids have passed the "operating test." Then allow them to use this station.

KEEPING IT GOING

- ● In whole group lessons using read aloud, model how to respond to books with a partner. Over time, move these same responding options into the Listening and Speaking station for students to practice when talking about texts with a partner. (See Section 3: Planning and Teaching for lesson ideas.)

What Are Some Signs *of* Success?

Cooperation, collaboration, and communication are keys to success at this station.

You'll want students to be accountable for using their time wisely at Listening and Speaking stations. Children may share with the class what they did/learned at the Listening and Speaking station during a five- to ten-minute class Reflection Time following stations/small group time. They may send a photo or recording to their teacher and/or family via an app like Remind, Seesaw, or Class Dojo.

Other indicators you'll notice when observing for successful Listening and Speaking stations include the following:

- Students are listening actively to a recording with a partner. They are seated (on the floor or in a chair) and are focused on what they are hearing and reading.

- Learners hold a book or device together and follow along as they listen.

- After listening, students respond together. They talk about the recorded book, perhaps using a conversation card, or write together in response to what they listened to. Students may use a graphic organizer to discuss story elements or text features that gave them information. (See Section 3: Planning and Teaching for specific ideas.)

- Children can tell you what they're doing at this station (e.g., *We are listening to informational text.*) and why (e.g., *We're learning new information about electricity, which we're studying in science. We're taking notes about what we learned to share with the class.*).

- Students put materials back neatly and in an organized way.

- Students can problem solve quickly when equipment malfunctions or materials cause confusion.

If you notice that students aren't doing what you expect at the Listening and Speaking station, bring them back to whole group and ask them what they should do differently to proceed. Don't accept behavior that isn't what you want to see. Reteach as needed. Use the Launch Lesson for the Listening and Speaking Station no matter the time of year!

TIME-SAVING TIP: Include a daily group Reflection Time to ensure smooth operation of stations. As children share what they've been practicing, you'll have a quick look at what you should do to support their learning at the Listening and Speaking station.

Troubleshooting Tips

Here are some tips to help you troubleshoot at the Listening and Speaking station, based upon my experiences in classrooms across North America over the years.

IF YOU NOTICE THIS	TRY THIS
Children get too loud.	Teach them to *remove* the headphones before they talk with each other.
Children interrupt the teacher because they need help with the equipment (headsets don't work, no internet connection, etc.).	Have a backup plan for what to do if technology isn't working. Develop this plan *with* your class and teach it well. For example, if the headphones don't work, they might read a book together instead.
Students waste time because they can't easily find the recording to listen to.	Use QR codes or organize links on a tablet dedicated for listening using Google Classroom or Symbaloo.
Students sit quietly and listen but don't respond to the text as expected or have conversations about it.	*Teach* (or reteach) students how to respond, scaffolding with conversation cards. Don't just put out sheets for kids to do to "prove" that they listened. (See Section 3 for ideas.)

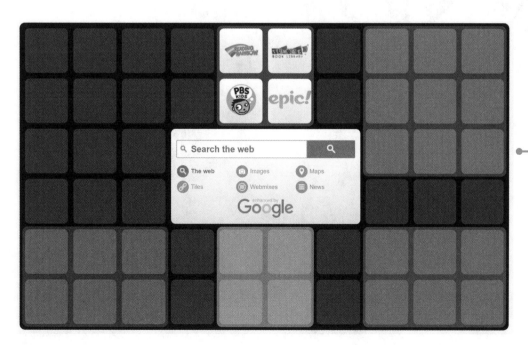

Symbaloo is one way to organize what students might listen to on a device.

Planning and Teaching

iStock.com/monkeybusinessimages

iStock.com/FatCamera

It's important to remember, as you're planning literacy instruction and practice with stations, that the ultimate goal is transfer. Literacy stations are not just time-filler activities to keep kids busy while you're meeting with small groups. Station work should be directly connected to your whole group instruction over time, which is directly connected to standards. It all ties together intentionally, by design and through your expertise as a teacher. Improving practice at literacy stations begins with solid instruction and established routines for ongoing practice.

Section 3 presents ideas for how to plan and teach strong lessons that students will eventually practice over and over again across a school year with a partner at the Listening and Speaking station. Each piece begins with explicit instruction centered on a *timeless literacy standard* related to listening and speaking. These standards may vary slightly in wording from state to state, but they all are pieces that will remain no matter where you're teaching or what the current education movement is. Please change the language slightly, as needed, to match the standards in your school system.

In this section, I've broken down five timeless literacy standards, one at a time, to focus on crucial literacy skills related to listening and speaking. You'll find suggestions for how to teach and model each skill during whole group and then move it to the Listening and Speaking station where students will practice together with a partner. Students will practice multiple times throughout the year to provide spiral review, recurring practice that helps students transfer learning.

When students show that they understand **what** to do, **how** to do it, and can tell **why**, it's time to move that work into the Listening and Speaking station. Be intentional, and the children you teach will be, too.

The more students work with these concepts over time, the deeper their learning will go, and the more apt they will be to remember what it is that you've been teaching.

Start *With* Solid Planning

Good instruction (and subsequent practice) begins with planning. I've seen the best results when teachers work together as a grade-level team to plan literacy instruction and connected practice at stations. Yes, it may seem time consuming, but you'll get more fluent the more you work together. Come to your team-planning meetings prepared. Look at your curriculum documents to get an idea of which standards are coming up in the next few weeks. Have formative and summative assessment data in hand to think about students' needs, too. Then plan together for big ideas based on your school, district, and state learning standards—and keeping your students' needs in mind—using suggestions from this section of this book. I've included tips for choosing model texts you might use when teaching. Think about what you've tried in the past, and share successes and things that didn't go so well (and why).

TIME-SAVING TIP: Save the Simply Stations Planning Tool charts you've designed and use them as a starting point to plan together year after year.

You might use a big piece of chart paper and markers to plan together. Or have someone type and project your planning chart onto a screen you can all see and access. Or work in a Google Doc or on your school's platform. Your choice! The Simply Stations Planning Tool (see the printable at **resources.corwin.com/simplystations-listening**) is purposely simple and customizable, but it's the best way I've found to teach with intention from standards through whole group and into stations. Of course, planning as a team provides consistency across your grade as you work together to create engaging lessons. But the Simply Stations Planning Tool can also be used individually if you're the only second-grade teacher in your school or if you want to try these ideas on your own before working with a group.

Planning as a team will save time, over time. When you collaborate, your plans will be stronger. Someone may have technology strengths, another may know children's literature well, and someone else may be good at creating visuals everyone can use. I've found that if you look carefully at your standards together, think about student needs, gather some good resources to model with, and put in the time to teach well, it pays off in the quality practice students do at the matching stations across the school year.

Simply Stations Planning Tool [Standards to Stations]

STANDARD WE'RE TEACHING	ACADEMIC VOCABULARY	WHOLE GROUP IDEAS	PARTNER PRACTICE AT LITERACY STATIONS
			_____ Station

I like to divide my planning chart into four columns as shown in the example below. Let's walk through the Simply Stations Planning Tool together.

- Column 1 is where we write our state standard in its entirety (so we don't skip parts we don't like). Use my *timeless standards* to get you started, and then fill in the language of your state standard to be precise.

- In column 2, make a bulleted list of the academic vocabulary you want to use when teaching. This is the same vocabulary you'll want students to use when they're practicing in stations, too! You can include this language on conversation cards that kids use in whole group and eventually at the Listening and Speaking station. Several conversation cards are included as printables at **resources.corwin .com/simplystations-listening**. Feel free to make your own, too, to reflect the academic vocabulary students should be using in *your* state or school system.

- Column 3 is where we jot down ideas for whole group teaching. Include text titles and ideas for anchor charts, lessons, and conversation cards here. (You'll find many ideas for column 3 in this section of the book!)

- Finally, we take what we've taught in whole group (column 3) and draw an arrow to move it to column 4 (Partner Practice at Literacy Stations) along with the name of the station it fits into. You'll notice that sometimes kids can use this work at the Listening and Speaking station and at the Partner Reading station, for instance. Don't you just love flexibility?

Here's an example of a Simply Stations Planning Tool planned by a team. Note the Listening and Speaking station ideas in column 4 and see how they grew from the standard through planning instruction. Use this as a model, and feel free to make it your own!

Simply Stations Planning Tool with four columns filled out by a team of Missouri kindergarten teachers. They worked together to plan how to teach story elements and eventually move this work to Partner Reading and Listening and Speaking stations.

Teach *for* Transfer

On the following pages, you'll find a number of Listening and Speaking station ideas, all based on timeless literacy standards, to help you implement meaningful student practice. Remember, the timeless literacy standards I've included here are composites of standards encountered across states; wording may differ from the literacy standards used in your state or district, but you'll be able to find your exact standard that matches the timeless standard concept. In other words, these are meant to be a starting point. I hope you'll use the ideas in this section as a springboard for other engaging station work throughout the year.

Each station idea centers on a timeless literacy standard and includes the following information to help you get started:

WHAT IT IS: This breaks down what the standard means to clarify what we want learners to understand. I've included the most important information we want students to know deeply and be able to apply over multiple increasingly complex texts.

WHY IT'S IMPORTANT: It's important for both students *and* teachers to understand why we're learning something. In today's world, with all its distractions and competition for attention, it's especially important for students to understand the "why."

MYTHS AND CONFUSIONS: Because I've been teaching for more than four decades, I've worked through many misunderstandings and confusions children (and sometimes teachers) have around skills and standards. So, I'm laying these out at the start to make you aware of problems that might occur and how to prevent them.

REAL-WORLD APPLICATIONS: This is sometimes referred to as "relevance." Children need to understand how they will be able to use this in the real world in order to help make their learning concrete and transferrable to other areas. This helps boost engagement, too.

You'll then find ideas for teaching for transfer in whole group and ways to move these concepts into station work for partners. I use the sequence of Plan, Teach, Practice, Reflect for each timeless standard:

1. **PLAN** thoughtfully (with your grade-level team if possible) to ensure student engagement and strong instruction. I've included sample texts to model with and key ideas to think about as you plan with a timeless standard in mind.

2. **TEACH** with intention. I've included sample anchor charts, conversation cards, graphic organizers, and tips to engage learners related to this timeless standard.

3. **PRACTICE** what's been taught at literacy stations (after students are familiar with the concept). Here you'll find grade-level adaptations for the timeless standard at this station and photos of what students at various ages can do at the Listening and Speaking station.

4. **REFLECT** with your class. This will keep literacy stations going as students share what they're learning. It will give you a day-to-day pulse on student practice with "paperless accountability" as children share what they've done.

Photos throughout show you possibilities for what the Listening and Speaking station can look like in your classroom, too.

TIMELESS LISTENING AND SPEAKING STANDARDS

1.	The student will describe and discuss characters and their interactions in a story.	Fiction
2.	The student will listen actively and ask questions.	Fiction/Nonfiction
3.	The student will listen for and use new vocabulary.	Fiction/Nonfiction
4.	The student will listen and follow directions to make or do something.	Nonfiction
5.	The student will listen and take notes/share important information.	Nonfiction

Timeless Listening and Speaking Standard 1

The student will describe and discuss characters and their interactions in a story.

Let's take a closer look at this timeless standard before we begin teaching and moving it into a Listening and Speaking station. Look closely at your own state standards for specific grade-level expectations and academic vocabulary. By teaching this standard well, children will have a deeper idea of what to listen for and speak about when they hear or (eventually) read stories on their own. By practicing at a Listening and Speaking station, learners will have the opportunity to hear a wide variety of stories over time and practice thinking and talking about characters with others.

What It Is

- Characters are the "who" in a story. In fiction, characters are made up but may be very much like people we know. Characters can be people or animals/creatures that act like people.

- There are main/major characters and minor/supporting characters in stories. Their relationships affect their behaviors.

- Characters may change throughout a story. Pay attention to events (and other characters) that influence changes.

- Comparing and contrasting characters aids comprehension within a story and across stories, especially in a series.

- Characters have feelings and traits (internal and external).

Why It's Important

- When readers pay close attention to characters, they understand the action of the story.

- Understanding characters helps readers predict and infer.

- Connecting to characters and their feelings helps readers comprehend why characters act like they do.

- Listening to stories and then discussing characters is a stepping stone to deeper understanding since listening comprehension precedes reading comprehension.

Myths and Confusions

- Young readers may have difficulty sorting out who is the main or most important character. Help them look at who the story is mostly about. Sometimes the story's title includes that character's name or the character is pictured on the front cover.

- Sometimes students confuse character feelings with traits. Help them identify character feelings as how characters feel at that point in the story and character traits as how characters act over time. Character feelings are often temporary, but character traits are long-lasting and part of that character's personality. A character trait is how someone acts no matter what happens to them.

- Model how to talk about how characters feel. Help children pay attention to a character's words, thoughts, and actions as you read aloud. Also help them pay attention to the illustrations and what the illustrator conveys by a character's facial expression and placement on the page.

- One of the biggest problems kids have is naming character traits. This is a great place to teach vocabulary. Post and refer to a list of character traits, developed with your class over time, to expand children's vocabulary and understanding as you teach them how to think and talk about characters. Printables are available on the companion website, **resources.corwin.com/simplystations-listening**. Students should be able to give text-based reasons for naming character traits, as these are often described or conveyed by dialogue or actions.

EL TIP: Post a familiar character from read aloud and add character traits around the picture to remind multilingual students of those words.

Character Traits List for Grade K–1

POSITIVE CHARACTER TRAIT	OPPOSITE
kind	unkind; mean
thoughtful	selfish
helpful	unconcerned
friendly	grumpy; grouchy
brave; courageous	cowardly
clever	foolish
patient	impatient
honest; truthful	dishonest; deceptive
curious	disinterested
pleasing; delightful	annoying; irritating
organized	disorganized; messy
successful	unsuccessful
respectful	disrespectful; rude
generous	greedy
ambitious	lazy
adventurous	cautious
calm	wild

Character Traits List for Grades 2–4

POSITIVE CHARACTER TRAIT	OPPOSITE
creative	dull
confident	anxious; nervous
agreeable	stubborn
responsible	undependable
eager	hesitant
athletic	clumsy
loyal; trustworthy	disloyal; fickle
certain	uncertain; confused
independent	reliant
forgiving	revengeful
bold; daring	timid; shy
hard-working	lethargic
cooperative	argumentative
humble	conceited
persistent	wavering
sympathetic	inconsiderate
assertive	unaggressive
perceptive	unobservant

Simply Stations: Listening and Speaking

Real-World Connections

- Characters in books can help us think about our own character. If we pay attention, we can learn lessons from characters in the books we read and listen to.

- When we tell stories about our lives, we talk about who (characters) and how we feel and act (feelings and traits).

- Listening to stories and discussing what we heard using examples from the text will help students develop conversation skills they will use their entire lives. This is critical today given the amount of screen time many young children have outside of school.

EL TIP: Include stories from the oral traditions of cultures matching your students. This will help multilingual children connect to characters and cultures that are familiar to them.

How Practice at the Listening and Speaking Station Helps Students

- As students *listen* to stories and pay attention to characters, they will start to understand how to *read* stories and pay attention to characters. Listening removes the cognitive load of reading. Learners are free to *think* about characters as they work at this station.

- Talking about characters can help learners share and clarify understanding of characters in stories they hear. Speaking also helps build language and communication skills.

EL TIP: Use conversation cards both in whole group and at the Listening and Speaking station to provide sentence stems for students who are learning a new language. This will also build academic vocabulary for all learners.

- Children can practice talking about character traits using evidence from stories they listened to. They can return to texts multiple times and listen for deeper understanding.

- The ability to listen and discuss what they've heard using examples from the text will help students develop conversation skills that will last throughout their lives! This interaction is especially important now that so many young children spend time watching or playing on personal devices at home.

It's important to teach concepts well in whole group before moving this work into the Listening and Speaking station. This will help students eventually know how to practice the same activities with a partner independently of you. Consider the following steps for whole group instruction to ensure student success with this standard.

1. Plan

Select Picture Books

Because you'll be modeling the listening and speaking work kids will do in the station, think about this standard and the kind of book that will help children understand the skill you're teaching. In this case, choose picture books with one memorable, strong character to start, especially in the early grades. Then move to books with main and minor characters and, over time, books with two or more main characters. To deepen understanding, look for books where characters change throughout. Provide the same types of books for children to work with at the Listening and Speaking station. Also look for books in a series, so students can use what they know about a character to make predictions, deepen comprehension, and compare characters' actions and adventures.

Here are a few book suggestions by grade level to get you started:

KINDERGARTEN	GRADES 1–2	GRADES 3–4
Pete the Cat series	*Elephant and Piggie* series	*Humphrey* series
No, David!	*Peter's Chair* and other books by Ezra Jack Keats	Books by Patricia Polacco
Duck and Goose	*Biscuit* books	*Judy Moody* books
Knuffle Bunny	*Rocket* books	*Magic Tree House* books with Jack and Annie
Little One Step	*Frog and Toad* series	
	Pedro: First Grade Hero series	

2. Teach

Co-Create Anchor Charts in Whole Group

Start with a read aloud of picture books; read it through the first day to enjoy the story, then on day two, start teaching about characters. Make an anchor chart with your class to help them pay attention to characters. Use academic vocabulary from your standard on the chart and highlight it in color. Add images of a few favorite characters from books to your chart as you read aloud books with these characters in them. Point to your anchor chart and encourage children to use this as a resource, too. Be sure kids are using the academic vocabulary, including *characters*.

I've included sample lessons for modeling, one for primary grades and another for intermediate grades, at the end of this section to help you get started.

Anchor chart on characters for kindergarten with characters added over time.

Second-grade anchor chart on characters made with *The Boy Who Cried Wolf*.

Third-grade anchor chart on characters reflects upper-grade academic vocabulary.

Introduce Novelty to Help Kids Pay Attention

- Use plush animals, if you have them, that represent main characters in stories. Pass the animal-character around the circle and have children tell something about that character. They might hold the animals as they listen to recorded books at the Listening and Speaking station. Big kids like stuffed animals, too! This isn't just for K–1.

- Print a drawing of a main character (and minor characters) from a story onto card stock and attach each to a ruler to create a stick puppet. (Or, have a student draw, color, and cut these out for the class to use.) Pass the stick puppets around as students describe and discuss main characters and their interactions. These stick puppets might later be used at the Listening and Speaking station as children talk about these characters after listening to a recorded story.

Students talk about characters with a plush animal representing that character in a whole group circle.

Students talk about characters printed on sticks at the Listening and Speaking station.

Use Conversation Cards to Develop Academic Vocabulary

I like to model with conversation cards in whole group to give children scaffolds for academic vocabulary I expect them to understand and use when speaking about characters. You can use these cards or adjust them slightly to reflect the exact academic vocabulary your state uses. Post them on the board in your whole group area and have kids use them when speaking about characters. Then move them to the Listening and Speaking station for students to use as they listen and then speak about characters in stories. The photos show sample conversation cards, and there are reproducible conversation cards at **resources.corwin.com/simplystations-listening**, too.

Sample conversation card from first grade.

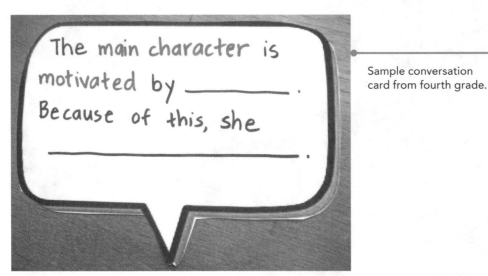

Sample conversation card from fourth grade.

Use Graphic Organizers for Response/Remembering

Many teachers use graphic organizers to help their students organize their thinking and remember what they read or listened to. Model, model, model with them before moving the same graphic organizers to the Listening and Speaking station for students to use with a partner. I often fill them out *with* students as they listen to a book read to improve comprehension and remind them *what* to listen for. Here are a few samples you might use for teaching in whole group and also at the Listening and Speaking station after kids are very familiar with them. You will find printable versions on the companion website, **resources.corwin.com/simplystations-listening**.

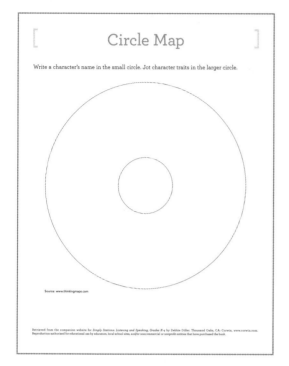

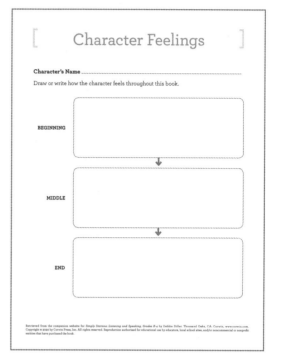

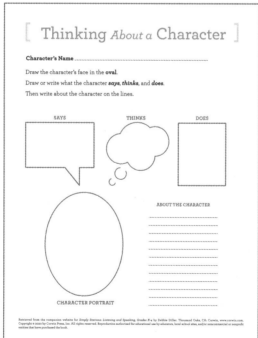

The following pages contain two sample lessons for modeling that you can use when teaching students about characters in whole group read aloud. One lesson is intended for primary grades; the other is for intermediate grades. You can use these as examples to get you started with whole group lessons that will then be transferred to partner practice at the Listening and Speaking station.

SAMPLE LESSON for MODELING WITH A READ ALOUD BOOK in PRIMARY GRADES

MODEL TEXT: *The Pigeon Finds a Hot Dog* by Mo Willems (simple, short book with a strong main character)

TIMELESS STANDARD: The student will identify and **describe** the **main character**. (Be sure this reflects your state and grade-level standards; adjust accordingly.)

TEACHER TALK:

- In this book, let's pay attention to the main character.
- Look at the illustrations of the character. What do you think he's feeling? Doing? How do you know?
- Listen to the words. Which words tell us what the character is feeling?

STUDENT TALK: Use the conversation card to demonstrate. This printable is available at **resources.corwin.com/simplystations-listening**. Kids will use these in whole group and at the Listening and Speaking station.

- The **main character**, _____, ...

LESSON STEPS:

The goal is for students eventually to understand how to describe main characters using details well enough that they can continue to do this without teacher assistance at the Listening and Speaking station.

1. Show the front cover and read the title. Have kids tell what they learn about the main character using the conversation card after you model its use. Repeat using the title page to learn more about the main character.

2. Read a few pages at a time, pausing to think aloud about the main character. (e.g., *Pigeon is talking about the yummy hot dog he will eat. He looks excited. The author used exclamation points. His wings are flapping. The illustrator made little lines to show this. His mouth is open wide. Uh, oh. Here comes Duckling. How is Pigeon feeling now?*)

3. Continue through the book, pausing at places where the action changes or kids can make a prediction about what will happen next, based on what they know about the main character.

4. After reading the book, pass around a stick puppet of the main character, inviting children to describe this character using events from the story as support. (e.g., *The main character, Pigeon, was hungry. He wanted to eat the hot dog. The main character, Pigeon, said the hot dog was a taste sensation. He was so excited to eat the hot dog. The main character, Pigeon, felt selfish and didn't want to share the hot dog.*)

QUICK ASSESS:

Did students describe the main character? What text evidence did they include from the words? The illustrations? What did they understand about the main character in this story?

AUTHOR'S CRAFT CONNECTION:

Use Author's Craft cards to help students think about what the author did to help us pay attention to characters. The goal is for students to understand this well enough that they can do this without teacher assistance at the Listening and Speaking station. A printable card for kids to use at the station is available at **resources.corwin.com/simplystations-listening**.

- How did the illustrator show what the main character was feeling? (e.g., eyes, mouth, lines to show action)

- What words did the author use that told what the main character was feeling?

- Why did the author use big, bold letters? End punctuation marks? Speech bubbles? What did that teach us about the main character?

WRITING CONNECTION:

If you incorporate writing into studying about characters, children may eventually be able to write about characters at the Writing station, too.

Model and then have students tell and write stories with a main character that shows feelings. They might use speech bubbles, end punctuation, or bold words. They might even write a story with the main character from the book.

MOVING THIS LESSON TO PARTNER PRACTICE AT A STATION:

At the Listening and Speaking station, have kids work with a partner using the same conversation cards and stick puppets from the lesson, but only after they show understanding of how to do this. They may need several models! They should listen to a recorded story with strong characters and then respond together.

SAMPLE LESSON for MODELING WITH A READ ALOUD BOOK in INTERMEDIATE GRADES

MODEL TEXT: *The Name Jar* by Yangsook Choi (more complex book with a strong main character)

TIMELESS STANDARD: The student will **describe** the **characters** in a **story**, including their **traits**, **motivations**, or **feelings**. (Be sure this reflects your state and grade-level standards.)

TEACHER TALK:

- The author introduces the main character from the start. What do you know about this character?

- How does this character feel at the beginning of the story? How do you know? Why does she feel that way? How does she feel at the middle of the story? At the end?

- What are this character's traits? How would you describe her personality?

- What/who motivated the character in this story? What did she do as a result?

STUDENT TALK: Use conversation cards to model the talk that's expected. Use reproducibles found at **resources.corwin.com/simplystations-listening**. Kids will use these at the Listening and Speaking station, too.

- The **main character**, _____, **feels** _____. **Text evidence is** _____.

- She shows the **character trait** _____. I know this because _____.

- The **main character** is **motivated** by _____. Because of this, she _____.

LESSON STEPS:

The goal is for students to eventually understand how to discuss main characters using details about character feelings and traits well enough that they can continue to do this without teacher assistance at the Listening and Speaking station.

1. Have the class read the front cover, the end papers, and the title page. Ask them to make predictions about the main character and a problem she may encounter in the story.

2. Read aloud a few pages at a time, pausing to think aloud with the students about the main character. Use the teacher talk and student talk ideas above. Start with character feelings.

3. You might draw a large circle map on the board and write the main character's name in the middle. (See the printable from **resources.corwin.com/simplystations-listening**.) Then jot down her feelings in the outer circle as students name these. Consider using a green marker to write feeling words from the beginning of the story, black for the middle, and red for the end.

4. Continue throughout the book, stopping at places where the action changes or kids can make a prediction about what will happen next, based on what they know about the main character.

5. Pause when Joey, another important character, is introduced, and make a second circle map about him.

6. At the end of the book, discuss each character's traits and their motivations. Use the character list on page 50 as a resource. Write the character traits around the outside of the circle map. Have students use conversation cards to help them use academic vocabulary.

QUICK ASSESS:

Did students describe the character's feelings accurately? Traits? Motivations and what she did as a result? What text evidence did they include from the words/illustrations? (Reflect on students' thinking about the main character and another important character in the story.)

AUTHOR'S CRAFT CONNECTION:

Use Author's Craft cards to help students think about what the author did to help us pay attention to characters' feelings and traits. The goal is for students to understand this well enough that they can do this without teacher assistance at the Listening and Speaking station. A printable card for kids to use at the station is available on the companion website, **resources.corwin.com/simplystations-listening**.

- How did the author tell the reader what the main character was feeling? (e.g., using words like *nervous, excited*; telling about her actions like *fingered the little block of wood in her pocket*)

- How did the illustrator show the main character's feelings? (her body's expressions, especially her eyes and hands)

- Look at the author's use of conversation in this story. Why do you think the author used so much dialogue? Was the whole story written in dialogue? Why not?

- Examine the author's use of italics in this story. Why do you think the author italicized those particular words?

WRITING CONNECTION:

If you incorporate writing into studying about characters, children may eventually be able to use what they've learned about characters as they write their own stories at the Writing station.

Model and then have students tell and write stories with a main character or personal narratives that show feelings. They might add some dialogue and/or italicized words in their stories, looking at the model text for ideas of where to include these things. Students might research and write a story about what their names mean and why they were given that name.

MOVING THIS LESSON TO PARTNER PRACTICE AT A STATION:

At the Listening and Speaking station, have kids work with a partner using the same conversation cards and the circle map from the lesson, but only after they show understanding of how to do this. They may need several models! They should listen to a recorded story and then respond together. They may also write stories incorporating what they've learned about characters into their own narratives.

---

3. Partner Practice

Once you see that students are able to describe and discuss characters and their interaction in a story, you're ready to move that same work into partner practice at the Listening and Speaking station. At first, learners will be doing the same thing that you've modeled during read aloud lessons. But over time, students can do more than simply listening to a recorded book at the Listening and Speaking station. Remember to focus on having students listen and then respond by *describing* and *discussing* characters with a partner. Here are some additional, grade-specific suggestions to help you think about the best things for your children to practice.

Kindergarten

- I like to have kindergarten students listen to recorded books where they can first view the story being acted out to engage them. It's important to have the matching book for them to look at, too, if possible. First have them listen and view with a partner. Then have them listen to the book, hold the book with a partner, and turn the pages to go with the story. Finally, have them turn the pages and retell the story orally looking at the pictures with a partner.

- Be sure to have students listen to books with just one strong character, so students can really focus on that character and what he or she is like.

- A simple stick puppet of just the main character (used in whole group) may help students talk about this character with a partner after listening. Provide a copy of the book students listened to, so they can reference the text as they talk.

Grades 1–2

- Stories will get more complex in Grades 1–2. There may be more than one main character. I like to use folk tales and fables in these grades. For example, there are the three little pigs and the big bad wolf. There are the tortoise and the hare, and the lion and the mouse.

- Having children talk about the characters will help them with retelling, too.

- Including visuals of the main characters may be helpful in getting kids to talk about the characters and act out how they act and feel. Have them use the main character puppets they used in whole group at this station.

- You might have partners work together to draw the setting on a piece of blank white paper to use with the characters.

- After students demonstrate understanding of how to use a circle map, have partners work together writing a character's name in the inner circle and jotting character traits in the outer circle.

Grades 3–4

- Students at these grade levels may still listen to picture books, but choose stories that are longer and more complex. Select books with characters that change over time.

- Third and fourth graders might also listen to recorded chapter books. These books take longer to finish but may help students access books they wouldn't normally read. You might have children go to the Listening and Speaking station several days in a row to give them time to finish listening to an entire book. You might have partners listen for fifteen minutes and then talk about what they heard for the last five minutes.

- Utilize graphic organizers with upper-grade students to help them think deeper as they listen. They might each take notes on an individual recording sheet as they listen but fill in a graphic organizer together as they discuss what they heard.

4. Reflect With Students

After your students have worked with this timeless standard at the Listening and Speaking station, reflect on what they've done here. Be sure to include a five- to ten-minute Reflection Time after stations where children can tell others what they've learned at this station. Section 4 of this book shows examples of templates you can use to jot down your ideas about the work you and your students did. Matching printables can be found on the companion website, **resources.corwin.com/simplystations-listening**.

Children may use the questions below to talk about the work that they did at the Listening and Speaking station during cleanup time. During Reflection Time, you can ask these questions again to learn more about what students did at this station today. (There are matching printables at **resources.corwin.com/simplystations-listening** that you can place at the Listening and Speaking station.)

1. What did you learn about a character at the Listening and Speaking station today?

2. What is one character trait a character showed in a story you listened to today? How did the author show this character trait?

3. How did the reader sound in a story you heard? Share how one of the characters sounded.

Timeless Listening and Speaking Standard 2

The student will listen actively and ask questions.

Let's examine this timeless standard before we begin teaching and moving it into a Listening and Speaking station. Look closely at your own state standards for specific grade-level expectations and academic vocabulary. By teaching this standard well, children will have a deeper idea of how to listen actively and speak or respond by asking questions when they hear or (eventually) read literary or informational text on their own. By practicing at a Listening and Speaking station, learners will have the opportunity to hear a wide variety of fiction and nonfiction over time and practice asking questions of each other about what they hear.

What It Is

- Hearing is a physical act; listening is a mental act.
- As we listen, we make meaning of what we hear and choose our response.
- An active listener does the following:
  - Looks at the speaker
  - Focuses on the message being communicated
  - Responds by summarizing or asking a question

Why It's Important

- People have a basic need to be heard/understood.
- When we listen actively, we are better able to understand and respond to people, situations, stories, and/or information.

- Listening comprehension precedes reading comprehension. If a child has trouble inferring about characters when text is read aloud, that student will most likely have difficulty inferring when reading independently.

- Asking questions can clear up confusions and propel readers forward.

Myths and Confusions

- Hearing and listening are not the same thing, but they are connected. Hearing involves sound waves; listening requires concentration. Remove physical distractions by seating children away from noisy HVAC units or windows with street/playground noise.

- Young children often confuse telling and asking. They may want to tell you a story about something when you want them to ask questions.

- Be explicit when teaching students to ask questions. Help them understand *why* we ask questions: to get information, not to *give* it!

- Model how to ask questions and name these as *questions* as you model.

EL TIP: Multilingual students may benefit from additional time at the Listening and Speaking station, especially if they can listen to books from read aloud that are recorded. Repeated listening will help to build language and comprehension.

Real-World Connections

- Active listening is important when interacting with others. Listening and asking questions helps build relationships and enables people to work better together.

- Listening builds language. Young children develop new vocabularies by listening and then trying some of the words they've heard; so do people learning a new language.

- Listening to recorded books or podcasts is a way people enjoy stories and learn new information. Look at the popularity of audiobooks, especially for adults with long commutes!

How Practice at the Listening and Speaking Station Helps Students

- Reminding students to *listen actively* to text and ask questions will build good reading and thinking habits. Listening removes the cognitive load of reading and allows learners to *think and ask questions* as they work at this station.

- Talking about their questions can help learners share and clarify understanding of what they listened to. You might teach younger students to pause the device when a question pops into their minds, so they can talk about it. Older students can jot down their questions on sticky notes and then talk about them after they have finished listening to the text.

- Thinking and asking questions can help students monitor their comprehension.

- Encourage children to also discuss answers to the questions they had. They may listen again to find answers using text evidence.

It's important to teach concepts well in whole group before moving this work into the Listening and Speaking station. This will help students learn how to practice the same activities with a partner independent of you. Consider these steps for student success with this standard.

1. Plan

Select Picture Books

Because you'll be modeling the listening and speaking work kids will do in the station, think about this standard and the kind of books that will help children understand the skill you're teaching. Choose picture books and articles (print and online versions) that will pique student interest when planning for instruction. Ask for children's input in what they'd like to learn about. They will be more focused (and listen actively) if they have a choice of what they listen to. Use the same types of recorded text at the Listening and Speaking station.

Look for books and articles that meet the following criteria when selecting text for active listening and asking questions.

EL TIP: Answering questions can help multilingual students listen with purpose. As you pair students at the Listening and Speaking station, you might give them roles. A native speaker could be the Questioner who asks questions, and a multilingual student could be the Answerer who answers the questions.

KINDERGARTEN	GRADES 1–2	GRADES 3–4
Text about experiences related to home or school	Books about things your students like to do, such as playing soccer or baseball	Books about topics of interest to your students
Books about things young children are naturally curious about (animals, weather, how things work)	Texts about topics your students want to know more about (e.g., how things work)	Literary texts with interesting characters kids can relate to and might wonder about
Informational books about topics of interest to your kids that have lots of photos and not too much text	Books with covers that might promote questions	Informational texts that have questions built into them through headings or other text features
	Informational text with headings in question form	Texts that answer students' inquiry/research questions

2. Teach

Co-Create Anchor Charts in Whole Group

Make an anchor chart on active listening *with* your class, including one with photos of your students. Label desired behaviors brainstormed with your kids. On another day, make an anchor chart about asking questions, including a list of question words. Post these where children can easily see them during whole group instruction. Review these charts before reading aloud to help children focus their attention. Here are some sample charts for inspiration.

Anchor chart on active listening.

Anchor chart on asking questions.

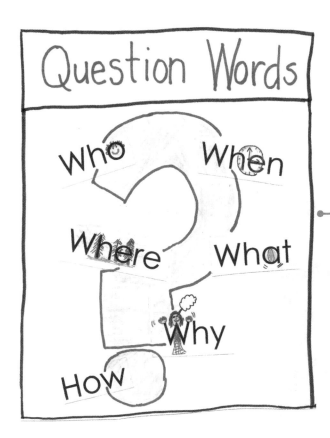

Anchor chart of question words.

Model How to Listen Actively and Ask Questions

Teach habits for active listening in read aloud and throughout the day. Give feedback directed toward students who are exhibiting active listening. (For example, *Manuel is watching the speaker. He is smiling at the funny parts, so I can tell he is listening.*)

Model how to ask questions at appropriate times during read aloud, such as when looking at the front cover of a book. Show how to read the title, look at illustrations, and ask questions that go with that book. Point to question words on your matching anchor chart as you encourage children to ask questions before, during, and after a read aloud.

I've included sample lessons for modeling at the end of this section to help you get started.

Use Signals to Help Kids Listen Actively

- Teach students how to look at the speaker and listen. To show they are ready to listen, they might point to their eyes and ears.

- They might also put their fingers to their lips to show "no interrupting" when someone is speaking.

EL TIP: Be sure students who are learning English as a new language sit near you when reading aloud (rather than on the outer edges of the group). Including them inside the group will encourage their participation during Turn and Talk time and give them "surround sound" as others share around them.

EL TIP: Be mindful of students who are in the early stages of learning a new language. Encourage them to use nonverbal signals, such as a thumbs up for "I agree" or a shrugging of the shoulders to show "I don't understand."

- Remind them to show emotion with their face/body to show they are listening. They might nod their head, smile, or move their body closer as they listen.

- During discussions, you might use hand signals to show active listening. (For example, a thumbs up means "I agree," or two fingers in the air means "I'd like to restate and add something.")

Students use thumbs up to show they agree, or they hold two fingers in the air to show, "I'd like to restate and add something."

Use Conversation Cards to Develop Accountable Talk

Show children how to be an active listener by using conversation cards for accountable (listening and) talk during read aloud. You might include some that are connected with a question on the left and a corresponding answer on the right to help children take turns and differentiate between asking and telling. Use these cards in whole group to teach student expectations. Eventually, you'll move these cards to the Listening and Speaking station for students to use as they listen and then share questions they have. They can also listen for answers as they work at the Listening and Speaking station together! (There are reproducible conversation cards available on the companion website, **resources.corwin .com/simplystations-listening**, similar to those shown on the next page.)

These connected conversation cards help students take turns asking questions and thinking about possible answers as they listen to stories.

EL TIP: Use conversation cards both in whole group and at the Listening and Speaking station to provide sentence stems for multilingual students. This will also build academic vocabulary for all learners.

Use Sticky Notes to Keep Track of Questions and Increase Active Listening

During read aloud, model how to jot down questions you have on sticky notes and place them on the page in the text where you had the question. Also show kids how to move the sticky notes to a place where that question is answered. Model how to jot questions on the cover, on pages in the book, and even on the back cover after you've finished reading. These questions may become the impetus for inquiry.

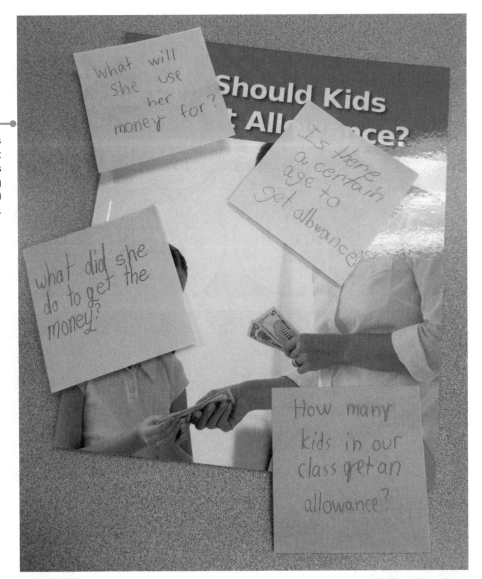

Questions students wrote on different colored sticky notes before (green), during (yellow), and after (pink) reading a text.

On the following pages are two sample lessons for modeling that you can use when teaching children about active listening and asking questions in whole group read aloud. One lesson is for primary grades, and the other is for intermediate learners. Please use these as examples to get you started with strong whole group lessons that will then be transferred to partner practice at the Listening and Speaking station. Use titles that will engage children and help them listen actively as well as prompt them to ask questions. Teach these lessons more than once and watch children become more active listeners and questioners. Substitute different text as you teach the lessons multiple times.

SAMPLE LESSON for MODELING WITH A READ ALOUD BOOK in PRIMARY GRADES

MODEL TEXT: *How to Make Bubbles* by Erika L. Shores (high-interest topic, simple procedural text)

TIMELESS STANDARD: The student will **listen actively** and **ask questions**. (Be sure this reflects your state and grade-level standards; adjust accordingly.)

TEACHER TALK:

- It's very important to listen actively, especially to directions.
- Asking questions helps us pay attention and get information.
- What do you want to know? What questions do you have?

STUDENT TALK: Use the conversation card to demonstrate. A matching printable is available on the companion website, **resources.corwin.com/simplystations-listening**. Kids will use these in whole group and at the Listening and Speaking station.

- My **question** is _____.

LESSON STEPS:

1. Before reading aloud, review active listening using an anchor chart. Show the front cover and read the title. Model how to ask questions, pointing to a question word chart. Use a sticky note with a large question mark on it to show where you have a question. If you work with students in Grades 1–2, jot down questions using the question word chart as reference.

2. Continue reading the book, pausing at places where you or your students have questions and jotting questions on sticky notes. (e.g., *Why must the water be warm? What is glycerin?*) Use teacher and student talk noted above. You might read part of the book one day and finish it on another. Watch your students to gauge their attention.

3. Read aloud the book again and have students work with you to follow the procedures in the book. Answer their questions if you can, moving the question sticky note to the spot where it is answered. If you don't find the answers, these may become inquiry questions to research. See the *Inquiry and Research Station* book in the Simply Stations series for further ideas.

EL TIP: Use texts that invite students to action, such as procedural texts. Setting a purpose for listening benefits multilingual students and all children, because they have something specific to listen for.

QUICK ASSESS:

Did students listen actively? Which listening behaviors are in place? Which need more time and practice? Did students ask questions? Do they understand the difference between asking and telling?

AUTHOR'S CRAFT CONNECTION:

Use Author's Craft cards to help students think like writers. The goal is for students to understand this well enough that they can do this without teacher assistance at the Listening and Speaking station. After they listen, have them use these to ask each other questions. See matching printables at **resources.corwin.com/simplystations-listening**.

- Why did the author include a table of contents? A glossary? An index?
- Notice that there's a materials list in photos near the start of the book. Why do you think the author used photos in this book instead of drawings?
- Why did the author write things in order in this book? What words show when or how to do things (e.g., *next, slowly, gently*)? What would happen if the pages came out and got mixed up?

WRITING CONNECTION:

If you incorporate asking questions into writing procedural text, children may eventually be able to practice writing procedural texts (using questions) as they work at the Writing station. Model, model, model!

Demonstrate how to write procedural text about something your class does on a daily basis (such as walking in the hallway or getting lunch). Create a title for the text that asks a question (*How Do We Walk in the Hallway? How Do We Get Our Lunch?*). Write each step on a separate page, modeling how to ask questions to think about what the reader needs to know next. For example, ask "What do we do after that? Why is it important?" Then mix up the pages and have students put them in order to make a book that tells things in order. Again, model how to ask questions about what you've written ("Is there anything else we should add?"). Eventually, children may write their own procedural texts about things they know how to do.

MOVING THIS LESSON TO PARTNER PRACTICE AT A STATION:

At the Listening and Speaking station, have kids work with a partner to listen to a recorded text. Give them sticky notes with large question marks on them to place when they have a question. Or, have them write their own questions on these sticky notes before, during, and after reading. Encourage students to talk with their partner about their questions (and find answers if possible). They might also talk about the author's craft of the book they listened to, using Author's Craft cards. Likewise, they might write procedural texts at the Writing station with a title that asks a question. Have them think about questions readers might ask as they write.

SAMPLE LESSON for MODELING WITH A READ ALOUD BOOK in INTERMEDIATE GRADES

MODEL TEXT: *The Little Red Pen* by Janet Stevens and Susan Stevens Crummel (a complex fiction or nonfiction book that evokes questions)

TIMELESS STANDARD: The student will **listen actively** and **ask questions** to **check understanding** of a speaker or a text. (Be sure this reflects your state and grade-level standards; adjust accordingly.)

TEACHER TALK:

- Listen actively to the speaker and to the text. What will help you do this?
- Asking questions can help you focus on the speaker and/or the text.
- Jotting down my questions helps me pay attention to what I'm reading.

STUDENT TALK: (Use matching printables from **resources.corwin .com/simplystations-listening**. Kids will use these at the Listening and Speaking station, too.)

- To **listen actively**, I …
- My **question** is _____?
- I'm not sure about _____. (ask a question here)

LESSON STEPS:

The goal is for students eventually to understand how to listen actively and ask questions well enough that they can continue to do this without assistance at the Listening and Speaking station.

1. Review active listening expectations with your class before reading aloud. Use the anchor chart you created with them. Then have students read the title and look at the front cover and title page. Model how to jot down questions you (or your students) have, one per sticky note, and place these on corresponding parts of the book.

2. Read aloud a few pages at a time, pausing to think aloud about what's happening in the story and articulating questions you have about the action. (For example, *What story is this reminding you of? What words does the author use to help the reader make this connection?*) Use the Teacher Talk and Student Talk ideas above. Also have kids turn and talk with a partner to share questions they have at selected places in the book.

3. As students share their questions, encourage active listening. Help students restate what a friend said or ask questions if they're unsure of what somebody wants to know or to check understanding of the text.

4. Move your sticky notes to places in the book where questions are answered (as you find answers together).

5. At the end of the book, have students tell questions they're asking now and have them explain how asking questions helped them understand the text.

EL TIP: Use books that have illustrations that support the text to increase understanding for students who are learning a new language. Encourage students to ask questions if they don't understand what the text means.

QUICK ASSESS:

Did students listen actively to the book and each other? Which listening behaviors are in place? Which need more time and practice? Did students ask questions to monitor their comprehension and clarify what others said? Did students ask questions that helped them understand the text and each other more deeply?

AUTHOR'S CRAFT CONNECTION:

Use the following to help students think about how the author used questions and other elements to craft the text to interest the reader. Then encourage children to think about doing the same as they write. The goal is for students to do this well enough so they can repeat this same kind of thinking at the Listening and Speaking station after listening to a recorded text. Use Author's Craft cards to guide and support student talk. A printable card for kids to use at the station is available on the companion website, **resources.corwin.com/simplystations-listening**.

- What got your attention in this book? What helped you to listen actively?

- How did the authors use questions in this book? Why do you think they used a question where they did?

- How is this story like *The Little Red Hen*? When and how did you figure that out?

- Examine the authors' use of color in this book. Why do you think they did this?

- What do you notice about the names of the authors? (*They are actually sisters!*)

WRITING CONNECTION:

If you incorporate asking questions into writing stories and other texts, children may eventually be able to practice doing this as they work at the Writing station.

Model and then have students tell and write stories that include questions to engage the reader. Students might want to experiment with using color or speech bubbles like the authors did in this book.

MOVING THIS LESSON TO PARTNER PRACTICE AT A STATION:

At the Listening and Speaking station, have kids work with a partner using the same conversation cards from the lesson and blank sticky notes to ask questions, but only after they show understanding of how to do this. They may need several models! They should listen to a recorded story and then respond together. They may also incorporate writing questions into the pieces they write at the Writing station.

3. Partner Practice

Once you see that children are able to listen actively and ask questions in whole group, you're ready to move that same work into partner practice at the Listening and Speaking station. At first, learners will be doing the same thing you've modeled during launching lessons. But over time, students should be able to extend this skill as they listen to all kinds of recorded texts. Here are some additional, grade-specific suggestions to help you think about the best things for you to model and for your children to practice at the Listening and Speaking station.

Kindergarten

- Little ones may have trouble focusing and listening actively, especially if they haven't been in formal school settings. Be clear about your expectations and give verbal directions for listening. For example, "*Look at the person speaking (or reading). Listen to what is happening in the story, so you can talk with your friends about it.*" Delay putting them in the Listening and Speaking station until you see that they can focus attention on listening in whole or small group. You might try using recorded books on YouTube that children may engage with more readily at first at the Listening and Speaking station.

- Five- and six-year-olds are big on telling stories instead of asking questions. In whole or small group, when they tell instead of ask, say, *"You are telling a story now. Try asking a question. My question is … or What happened …?"* Teach question words and post a small version of the question word anchor chart at the Listening and Speaking station to remind them to ask questions and not tell stories.

- You might use sticky notes with bold black question marks on them (instead of jotting down actual questions) when modeling asking questions. Have kids use these same prepared sticky notes at the Listening and Speaking station to show where they had questions. Be sure they stop and ask questions of each other. Again, post and remind them to point to question words on a small version of the question words anchor chart.

Grades 1–2

- As stories get longer, you might see children's active listening falter. Pay attention to your children when reading aloud to them. Be sure they are listening before continuing with a book. If interest wanes, try acting out a part or asking them to chime in on a repeating or predictable part. Remind them of your expectations for active listening and why this is important. As they work at the Listening and Speaking station, tell children to join in on the repeating or predictable parts, too. If you do this, you might teach kids how to listen without headphones. Teach them how to control the volume (of the recording and their voices!). Place a colored sticker on the books with repeating/predictable parts to remind students to join in.

- Six- and seven-year-olds may still confuse asking and telling. Be persistent. Use suggestions from the kindergarten section above.

- Model how to use the connected conversation cards (found on the companion website, **resources.corwin.com/simplystations-listening**) to encourage partners to ask and answer questions. Begin in whole group during read aloud with turn and talk. Be sure students can use these well before moving the cards into the Listening and Speaking station. Remind them to use the cards before they begin stations. Occasionally, ask children to tell about conversation cards they used here during Reflection Time at the end of stations.

- Having a copy of the question words anchor chart at the Listening and Speaking station may remind children to ask questions. It will also provide a model for how to spell these words when kids are jotting down questions as they listen to recorded books at the Listening and Speaking station.

Grades 3–4

- Students at these grade levels should be improving in active listening, but some may still need reminders of how to listen. It's important for you to only give directions (or say something) one time in whole group. Let students know this is your norm and that you expect them to listen actively. Give one direction and have kids do this task before giving the next direction.

- Use an anchor chart for accountable talk and conversation cards from this book to help students with active listening both in whole group and at the Listening and Speaking station.

- Provide blank sticky notes at the Listening and Speaking station for kids to use as they listen to recorded books or podcasts. Have them jot down questions they have as they listen. Teach them how to share their questions with their partner after listening and how to help find answers to questions, too.

- Continue to model how to listen actively and ask questions in upper grades. You might keep an ongoing list on a bulletin board or display space of open-ended questions your students have generated, especially related to social studies and science during whole group. Invite students to add to this list after asking questions at the Listening and Speaking station, too. Eventually, these may become research topics your students want to investigate.

- Invite older students to create recordings of books that invoke questions for their peers to listen to at the Listening and Speaking station. You might convert this station into a Recording Studio. See page 154 for more information.

4. Reflect With Students

After your students have worked with this timeless standard at the Listening and Speaking station, reflect on what they've done here. Be sure to include a five- to ten-minute Reflection Time after stations where children can tell others what they've learned and done at this station. Section 4 of this book shows samples of forms you can download from the companion website, **resources .corwin.com/simplystations-listening,** to jot down your ideas about the work you and your children did.

Students may use the questions below to talk about the work that they did at the Listening and Speaking station during cleanup time. During Reflection Time, you can ask these questions again to learn more about what students did at this station today. (There are matching printables at **resources.corwin.com/ simplystations-listening** that you can place at the Listening and Speaking station for readers to use.)

1. Were you an active listener at the Listening and Speaking station today? What did you do that helped you listen actively?

2. What was a question you asked while listening to a text at the Listening and Speaking station today? Did you find the answer to your question? What was the answer?

3. What did you notice today at the Listening and Speaking station about how authors used questions in their books? How can you try that in your writing?

This anchor chart reminds students of things to say when listening actively and having discussions.

Accountable Talk
(BE RESPONSIBLE!)

- "I agree with what ___ said."
- "I disagree, because ___."
- "I have something to add to what ___ said."
- "In my opinion, ___."
- "Why do you think that?"
- "Will you give me an example?"

Timeless Listening and Speaking Standard 3

The student will listen for and use new vocabulary.

Let's take a look at this timeless standard before we begin teaching and moving it into a Listening and Speaking station. Look closely at your own state standards for grade-level expectations and academic vocabulary. By teaching students how to listen for and use new vocabulary, they will have a better understanding of what they hear or read. Instead of just skipping over words they don't know the meanings of, students will learn how to stop and figure out the definition of those words in the context of listening and looking or reading. By practicing at a Listening and Speaking station, learners will have the opportunity to hear a wide variety of texts read to them with new vocabulary and think about those new words and their meanings.

What It Is

- Vocabulary refers to the words that make up a language. There are basic words that we use in everyday conversation (e.g., *happy, door, ran*); there is more sophisticated language used by people with more mature speech (e.g., *elated, portal, dashed*); and there are content-specific words used mostly in those disciplines (*decimal, archipelago, fossil*).

- Vocabulary encompasses understanding synonyms, antonyms, idioms, homographs, and homophones as students' literacy learning advances.

- Studying affixes (e.g., *pre-, un-, -ly,* -ful) can help children understand new words as they encounter these in text.

- Learning to use print and digital resources, such as dictionaries and thesauri, can also help children learn meanings of new words.

- It's important to teach children how to figure out the meaning of any word they don't understand. Begin by having them stop and ask, *"What's that word mean?"* when comprehension breaks down because of vocabulary.

EL TIP: Focus on cognates when working with students who are learning English as a new language. Helping them understand how words from their home language connect to English words will quickly help to build vocabulary. For example, many words are the same in English and Spanish (e.g., *hospital, gas, animal*). Google "most common cognates" for words that fit in this category.

Why It's Important

- Knowing what words mean is critical for comprehension. New vocabulary load increases as reading levels become more advanced.

- Children learning a language (especially young children or students learning English) must learn new words and their meanings, or vocabulary will become a stumbling block that prohibits them from fully understanding what they've listened to (or read).

- Well-developed oral language/vocabulary is strongly associated with later reading proficiency.

Myths and Confusions

- I often see teachers "pre-teach" vocabulary by showing flash cards of the hard words in a book before children read that book. Although we may think we've "taught" these new words, this may not be the most effective way to help children learn vocabulary.

- Giving kids a list of vocabulary words to memorize doesn't usually make those words stick. Students need to see/hear/work with a new word many times (ten to twelve iterations) in rapid succession in a meaningful context to learn that word.

- Simply being read to isn't enough. Adults should model how to figure out word meanings (e.g., by using a picture or other words around the new word). Kids need to be involved in rich discussions about new words and encouraged/supported to use those words orally.

- Teach children to *listen for* new vocabulary. This is the first step in helping them learn new words. Listening vocabulary develops first; then comes oral vocabulary, followed by reading and writing vocabularies.

EL TIP: An effective strategy for students learning a new language is to pre-teach vocabulary using real objects, role-playing or pantomiming, gestures, or pictures.

Real-World Connections

- People with higher-level vocabulary are typically perceived as intelligent and well-read. Often they have developed this vocabulary from wide reading and paying attention to new words.

- Helping your students develop vocabulary and become word lovers will reap benefits as they better understand what they read. Their writing may improve, too.

How Practice at the Listening and Speaking Station Helps Students

- With scaffolding and strong instruction, students *listen* to texts with new vocabulary and figure out and discuss the meaning of those words as well as the whole text. Listening removes the task of decoding, which can free learners to think about what the new words mean.

- Students get the chance to practice strategies for determining the meaning of new words with the support of a partner.

- Talking about new words and their meanings can help learners clarify, understand, and use new vocabulary.

- Using the new words from the listened-to text can develop language and improve comprehension of future texts read, especially those with the same words.

EL TIP: Provide real objects used in whole group read alouds with the same text for students to listen to. Include a 3-x-5 white index card with each new word written on it in black ink. Learners can match objects to the word cards. These cards can remind students learning a new language of the words to listen for and use as they discuss the text after listening. Then place these same texts and realia at the Listening and Speaking station for additional practice.

Realia and matching word cards accompany the book, *The Carrot Seed*, to provide support for vocabulary learning in whole group and later, at the Listening and Speaking station.

It's important to teach concepts well in whole group before moving this work into the Listening and Speaking station. This will help students to eventually know how to practice the same activities with a partner independent of you. Consider the following steps for whole group instruction to ensure student success with this standard.

1. Plan

Select Picture Books — and Words

Because you'll be modeling the listening and speaking work kids will do in the station, think about your students, this standard, and the kind of book that will help children learn new vocabulary. Consider what your students need, reflecting on their current levels of oral language. Think about their receptive language (what they hear and understand) as well as their expressive language (the words they use when speaking). Choose picture books with some new words, but not too many.

I like to select five to seven new words per book to focus on in read aloud. These words should connect to words kids already know and be used by people with more mature speech. It's a bonus if these words can be used when retelling the gist of the text. Write each of your selected words on a card or chart, post them on the board, and read them to the class.

Look for text that will help students determine the meaning of new words (such as illustrations that show what the vocabulary means; bold words and a matching glossary). (See lesson ideas on pages 90 and 93 for samples of vocabulary to choose from picture books.)

Here are some things to look for when reading aloud and choosing recorded books for the Listening and Speaking station with new vocabulary at varying grade levels:

KINDERGARTEN	GRADES 1–2	GRADES 3–4
Clear illustrations that match new words	Not too many new words per page	New words that can be figured out by using words/sentences around the new word
Higher-level vocabulary that corresponds with simple words kids already use (*exclaimed/said*; *overjoyed/happy*).	Idioms that can be figured out easily	Idioms and book language; homonyms, homophones, homographs
Simple labels in nonfiction books that match new vocabulary	Multiple-meaning words with new uses and picture support	Bold words and other text features that aid in vocabulary understanding in nonfiction (e.g., labels, glossaries, vocabulary boxes)
	Bold words and labels in nonfiction	
	Bold words followed by dashes and definitions in nonfiction	
	Glossaries in nonfiction	

2. Teach

Model in Whole Group Read Aloud

Read aloud is a great place to model how to *listen for* new words. There are many ways to approach vocabulary teaching, but I'm going to focus on just a few to get you started.

Point to the words you've posted on the board. Tell students to *listen for* the words, because they're cool new words that will help them retell the book. Develop a signal with your kids to use when they hear these words (e.g., touch your ears, put your hands on your head) before reading.

Then read the book and pause when kids hear each new word. Help them figure out the meaning of each word by looking at the picture, inserting another word that makes sense there, or acting out what's happening. At the end of the read aloud, review each word by having kids tell or act out what it means. Encourage kids to use those words constantly while speaking and writing.

Here are more ways to model new words:

- Teach students to *listen for* new words in a read aloud. Have them make a "stop" gesture with their hands and say, "Stop. What does that word mean?" when they hear a word whose meaning they don't know. Be prepared to stop and help them figure out these words as you read aloud.

- Read aloud nonfiction books with text features that lead to new vocabulary learning. Model how to pay attention to bold words, simple labels, and glossaries to learn new words.

EL TIP: Have multilingual students act out new words to help them understand and remember the meaning of these words as they use their bodies to learn.

This anchor chart helps K–1 students pay attention to new words and think about what they mean. It's used in whole group and at the Listening and Speaking station.

Students use motions to show they wonder what a new word means during read aloud. This helps them listen for new words and think about their meanings.

Use Anchor Charts to Teach Concepts

Make an anchor chart about how to figure out the meanings of new words *with your class*. You might make one for fiction books and another for nonfiction books, as pictured below. Add ideas to the chart as you demonstrate how to try each strategy while reading books together in read aloud and shared reading. Include examples/visuals to help students remember.

Sample anchor chart for figuring out meanings of new words in fiction.

Sample anchor chart for determining word meanings in nonfiction.

Students Can Keep Track of New Words

When working with younger children, hand motions related to new words work well. Have kids touch their ears when they hear a new word, act out new words, or ask, "What's that word mean?"

Select a read aloud book that has new words in it that kids may be unfamiliar with but are supported by the text/illustrations. Prepare a grid with two blank squares across and two down, for a total of four blank squares. Model how to jot down a new word from the book at the top of each square when you come to it. Discuss the meaning of the word. A student might sketch a quick picture to go with it, too. A printable that is used at the Listening and Speaking station can be found at **resources.corwin.com/simplystations-listening**. (You might change this to a 3-x-3 grid for older students to provide space for more words.)

Students listen for new words and fill in a 2 x 2 grid at the Listening and Speaking station. Notice the space for them to illustrate each word, too. This is used in whole group first.

Older students might use highlighting tools to mark new words. If they have paper copies to listen to, they can use a highlighter pen to mark words that are new to them (or words whose meanings they're unsure of). Or, give them small pieces of highlighter tape attached to an index card. Direct them to place a small piece of tape over new words.

Some children might like keeping a word journal where they jot down new words they want to use in their writing someday. They might use a 3-x-5 notebook for this purpose. Or they might have a section of a writer's notebook or interactive reading journal tabbed with a section to list new words they find.

Use Graphic Organizers for Response/Remembering

The Frayer Model is probably the best-known graphic organizer for helping kids learn new words. The Frayer Model asks students to identify key characteristics, examples, non-examples, and a definition, but younger students or multilingual learners might benefit from drawing a representation of the word, too. Try modeling with a Frayer Model graphic organizer during read aloud and show students how to use this to dig deeper into the meaning of a new word. (You can find a printable Frayer Model graphic organizer on the companion website, **resources.corwin.com/simplystations-listening**.)

Frayer Model used by primary students at the Listening and Speaking station to listen for new words.

Third graders use the Frayer Model for vocabulary learning in a clear plastic sleeve with dry erase supplies at the Listening and Speaking station.

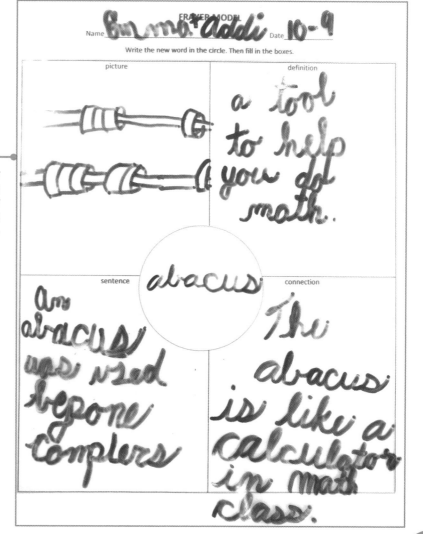

FRAYER MODEL

Name Emma + Addi Date 10-9

Write the new word in the circle. Then fill in the boxes.

picture

definition

a tool to help you do math.

abacus

sentence

An abacus was used before computers

connection

The abacus is like a calculator in math class.

The following pages contain two sample lessons for modeling to use when teaching students how to listen for and figure out the meaning of new vocabulary in whole group. Meaningful practice takes place at the Listening and Speaking station only if students know clearly what you expect them to do.

One lesson is intended for primary grades, and the other is for intermediate grades. You can use these as examples to get you started with whole group lessons modeling skills that will then be transferred to partner practice at the Listening and Speaking station. Please use titles that match the needs and cultures of your students as you teach these lessons. (Be on the lookout for texts with cognates if you teach native Spanish speakers.) I included sample texts for modeling and hope you'll teach these lessons multiple times with a variety of read alouds that introduce children to lots of new vocabulary over time.

SAMPLE LESSON for MODELING WITH A READ ALOUD BOOK in PRIMARY GRADES

MODEL TEXT: *City Dog, Country Frog* by Mo Willems (a short book with a few new vocabulary words)

TIMELESS STANDARD: The student will **listen** for and use **new words**. (Be sure this reflects your state and grade-level standards.)

VOCABULARY: *spotted, involved, croaking, admire, sniff*

TEACHER TALK:

- Listen for new words. Ask what they mean.
- Look at the illustrations for help.
- Try another word that makes sense.

STUDENT TALK: (Use matching printables on the companion website, **resources.corwin.com/simplystations-listening**. Kids will use these at the Listening and Speaking station, too.)

- My **new word** is _____. It means _____. I know this because _____.

LESSON STEPS:

1. Read the book one day for enjoyment; on another day, read the book again and tell children you want them to listen for new words they will learn to use.

2. Show them how to make a "stop" gesture with their hands, and say, "Stop. What does that word mean?" when they hear a word and

don't know its meaning. You might jot each new word on a white 3-x-5 index card with a thick black marker as students ask about it. Add a quick sketch to help them remember its meaning and place the card on the board. (Prepare a few of these ahead of time, as you may be able to anticipate the words you think kids will ask about.)

3. Help children figure out what each new word means as you're reading. Prompt them to substitute another word in its place that makes sense (e.g., *saw* for *spotted*) or look at the illustration for help (e.g., *sniffing*: the picture shows the dog's nose in the air). Make a simple anchor chart like the sample on page 85 of this book to remind kids what to try.

4. Encourage students to use the new words as they talk about the book. (e.g., City Dog *spotted* a frog, and they became friends. City Dog *sniffed* and Country Frog *croaked*.)

5. Use the new words often across the next few weeks at school. (e.g., I *admire* that blue sweater you're wearing.)

QUICK ASSESS:

Did students stop and ask about new words? How did they figure out the meanings of new words? Did they use the anchor chart for help? Were they able to discuss the book using the new words? Are they using the new words in their oral language or even their writing?

AUTHOR'S CRAFT CONNECTION:

Use Author's Craft cards to help students examine and use new vocabulary as they look more closely at the books they listened to. (A printable can be found at **resources.corwin.com/simplystations-listening**.) The goal is for students eventually to understand how to look for and use new vocabulary well enough that they can continue to do this without teacher assistance at the Listening and Speaking station. In this book, student talk might focus on how the illustrator used color. You might have them use new words related to color as they discuss.

- What main colors did the illustrator use? Why do you think he used these colors? (You might display a chart of shades of blue or green with the color names on it for reference.) Support and encourage kids to use advanced vocabulary to talk about the book's illustrations using color words, such as *Kelly green*, *citron*, *sky blue*, and *indigo*.

- Notice the seasons of the year in this book and how they are in order. Also look at the words naming seasons and their colors. Discuss why the author chose these colors (e.g., *Spring is written in pink like the tree blossoms in that season*.)

EL TIP: Provide a visual palette with color words written in boxes of those colors to expand vocabulary. Place this at the Listening and Speaking station for kids to use over time as they talk about author's (and illustrator's) craft.

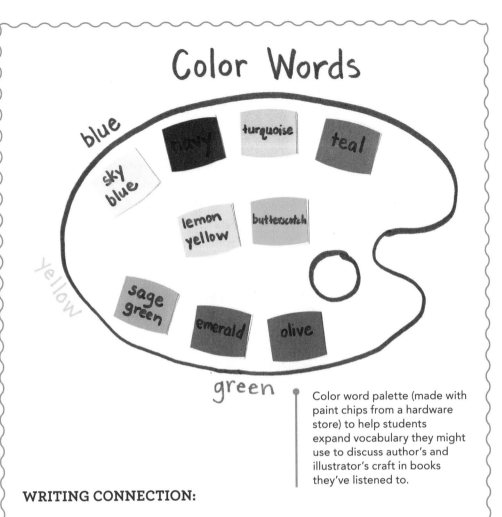

Color Words

blue

sky blue · navy · turquoise · teal

lemon yellow · butterscotch

yellow

sage green · emerald · olive

green

Color word palette (made with paint chips from a hardware store) to help students expand vocabulary they might use to discuss author's and illustrator's craft in books they've listened to.

WRITING CONNECTION:

Response writing is included in most state standards and curriculums. Writing a response to recorded text can help students deepen their understanding. In whole group, model how to write a response to this book using pictures and words. Incorporate new vocabulary from the story. Think aloud and have students help you craft this message. Invite students to talk and write their own responses to books read aloud, too. You might place this and other read aloud books at the Writing station and include response writing as an option for meaningful work here.

MOVING THIS LESSON TO PARTNER PRACTICE AT A STATION:

At the Listening and Speaking station, have kids work with a partner to listen to a recorded text. Have them listen for new words. Teach them how to use the pause button to stop and talk with their partner when they hear a new word. (Be sure to model this well! And if students are wearing headphones, teach them to remove these when talking.)

If you provide recorded books you've read aloud, include the word cards created for them to use (with picture support) to talk about the book after listening. They might also talk about colors in the books they've listened to, using some of their new color word vocabulary.

SAMPLE LESSON for MODELING WITH A READ ALOUD BOOK in INTERMEDIATE GRADES

MODEL TEXT: *Going Home* by Eve Bunting (more complex fiction or nonfiction book with higher level vocabulary, including multiple-meaning words)

TIMELESS STANDARD: The student will **listen** for and use **multiple-meaning words** to comprehend and discuss a **text**. (Be sure this reflects your state and grade-level standards.)

VOCABULARY: *sparkle, slides, battered, scattering, choke, lie, border, papers* (these are all words with multiple meanings)

TEACHER TALK:

- Listen for new words and new meanings. Don't skip over them!
- Listen for words you know, but that might have a different meaning in this text.
- Stop and think if something doesn't make sense. Maybe that word has a new meaning.

STUDENT TALK: (Use matching printable at **resources.corwin.com/ simplystations-listening**. Kids will use these at the Listening and Speaking station, too.)

- _____ is a **multiple-meaning word**. It means _____ here. It can also mean _____.

- A **new meaning** for _____ is _____. Another definition for this word is _____.

LESSON STEPS:

1. Read the title of the read aloud book with your class. Ask them what the words *Going Home* make them think of. Tell them that in this book it's different than just going to where they live after school. Sometimes words we think we know well have other meanings, too. Those are called *multiple-meaning words* and have more than one meaning.

2. Ask kids to help you listen for and make a chart of multiple-meaning words from this book and others they read. The more they pay attention to these kinds of words, the more their vocabulary will grow. Have a large piece of chart paper handy to jot down multiple-meaning words.

EL TIP: Ask multilingual students to add a quick sketch to your chart to help the class remember the multiple meanings of a word. This will help everyone, but especially the one who makes the drawing!

3. Read aloud, pausing when students hear a word with more than one meaning. For example, on page 1, *sparkle* is used to denote excitement. Jot this word on your chart and add quick sketches to show its meaning. Ask kids if *sparkle* can mean anything else (e.g., *a ring can sparkle; sparkling water is bubbly*). Make a quick sketch to go with these other meanings, too.

4. Read and think aloud about the story, pausing and jotting down other multiple-meaning words.

5. At the end of the book, ask students to retell the story using some of their new multiple-meaning words. Encourage them to use these words throughout the day/week/month, too.

Multiple-meaning word chart made with an intermediate class during whole group read alouds.

QUICK ASSESS:

Did students stop and think about multiple-meaning words? How did they figure out these new meanings? Were they able to discuss the book using the multiple-meaning words? Are they using the multiple-meaning words in their daily lives? Are they finding multiple-meaning words in other books, too?

AUTHOR'S CRAFT CONNECTION:

Looking at text through the lens of a writer can help students develop deeper comprehension and use some of these same techniques as they write. Use Author's Craft cards to help children closely examine how the author crafted this text by using certain words. (A reproducible can be found at **resources.corwin.com/simplystations-listening**.) The goal is for learners to understand this well enough that they can do this without teacher assistance at the Listening and Speaking station. Here are some questions you might ask about the author's word choice:

- What descriptive words did the author use that helped you visualize a scene in this book? (e.g., *sparkles with excitement*; *battered cooler*; *sun-filled winter sky*).

- Look at the font the author used. Why do you think the author chose this for the words?

- Notice that the author chose some Spanish words, but most of the text was in English. Why do you think the author did this? Why did she choose those particular Spanish words?

- The author uses the word *opportunities* often in this book. What does *opportunities* mean? Why do you think she repeated this word?

WRITING CONNECTION:

Demonstrating how to use multiple-meaning words in writing can help students learn to experiment with new vocabulary as they write at the Writing station. Model how to use multiple-meaning words and higher-level vocabulary as you write in front of your students. Encourage them to do the same as they write independently. Have them listen for and use some of the new words (and multiple-meaning words) with their classmates.

MOVING THIS LESSON TO PARTNER PRACTICE AT A STATION:

At the Listening and Speaking station, have kids work with a partner using the same conversation cards from the lesson and listen for/ discuss new words, but only after they show understanding of how to do this. They may need several models! They should listen to a recorded story and then respond together. Place the multiple-meaning chart near where they work and allow them to add new words to it if they hear some in their recorded books. Encourage them to use multiple-meaning words as they write at the Writing station, too.

3. Partner Practice

After you see that students are able to listen for new vocabulary (including multiple-meaning words) and decipher what those words mean in whole group lessons, it's time to move that same work into partner practice at the Listening and Speaking station. This will expand the listening experience into vocabulary-growing work embedded in meaningful text. At this station students should be listening for new words (and multiple-meaning words) and having discussions using these words in response. Here are some additional, grade-level specific suggestions to help you think about the best things for learners to practice at the Listening and Speaking station:

Kindergarten

- Little kids LOVE big words and will take on new vocabulary readily if you approach new words in a kinesthetic way. Remind them to act out the words as they talk about them at the Listening and Speaking station.

- Choose books carefully and focus on just a few new words per book, both in read aloud and at the Listening and Speaking station. Use recorded versions of books from read aloud at this station. You might make an 8.5-x-11 card for each book read aloud (for new vocabulary) for kids to use at the Listening and Speaking station. Include a thumbnail cover of the book with the new words listed in large black print. Beside each word, add a picture to show what it means. Ask kids to listen for these new words and then talk to each other about the words in the book.

- Later add the card to a vocabulary board display. Encourage kids to use these words in their writing at the Writing station, too.

Grades 1–2

- Choose five to seven words per new book as you focus on vocabulary in read aloud and shared reading. Model how to read the words around each new word to figure out what it means. Pictures can still help, too. Use the suggestion from kindergarten above for a vocabulary reminder to go with favorite read aloud books that kids can also use at the Listening and Speaking station. Or place the new words at the Writing station and invite children to write their own piece using some of those words.

- Provide a blank grid kids can use to listen for new words. (There's a printable at **resources.corwin.com/simplystations-listening**.) Don't always give them the new words. Have them listen for words that are new to them. Always provide space for the word and space beside it to tell or show what it means (with words or pictures). Move this to the Listening and Speaking station for kids to use independently. Have kids share their list with a partner after listening. Did they hear any of the same words? What new words did they learn?

- Provide a simple dictionary that you've modeled for children to use if they need help with some of the words.

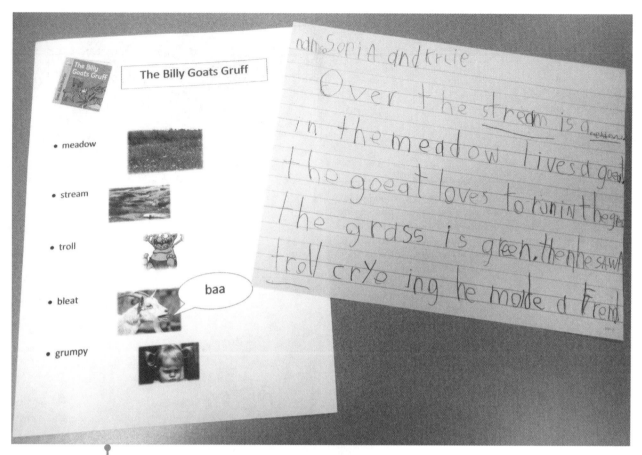

First graders use new some words from *The Three Billy Goats Gruff* to write their own story at the Writing station after listening to this book and using the word chart at the Listening and Speaking station.

Grades 3–4

- Adapt ideas for Grades 1–2 in upper grades. Students might add illustrations to a new word chart to go with a book they're listening to.

- Older students can use a blank Frayer Model to listen for new words and then demonstrate their meanings. (A printable is provided at **resources .corwin.com/simplystations-listening**.) After working with this in whole group, move this kind of work to the Listening and Speaking station.

- Ditto for idioms, multiple-meaning words, or homophones/homographs/homonyms.

- If students have word journals, let them use these at the Listening and Speaking station to jot down new words they hear. Be sure they talk with their partner about these new words after listening to a recorded selection.

Support for listening to a familiar book from read aloud at an upper-grade Listening and Speaking station includes a card with the new vocabulary to listen to and picture support added by students. It's later used at a Writing station, too.

The same vocabulary chart might be placed at the Writing station over time for kids to use as support for using those same words in writing.

Intermediate learners jot down new words in a community journal shared by the class at a Listening and Speaking station.

4. Reflect With Students

After your students have worked with this timeless standard at the Listening and Speaking station, reflect on what they've done here. Be sure to include a five- to ten-minute minute Reflection Time after stations where children can tell others about new words they've learned at this station. Section 4 of this book shows samples of forms you can download from the companion website, **resources.corwin.com/simplystations-listening**, to jot down your ideas about the work you and your children did with vocabulary.

Here are a few questions you might have students use to discuss the vocabulary they learned about at the Listening and Speaking station during cleanup time (with older readers). During Reflection Time, you can ask these questions again to learn more about what students did at this station today. There are matching printables at **resources.corwin.com/simplystations-listening** that you can place at the Listening and Speaking station if you work with intermediate students.

1. What is a new word that you heard at the Listening and Speaking station today? What did it mean? How did you figure it out?

2. What book did you listen to at the Listening and Speaking station today? Tell us something about the book using a new word or two from the book.

3. Summarize what you listened to today at the Listening and Speaking station. Use one or two of the new words you heard. (use this with intermediate students)

Timeless Listening and Speaking Standard 4

The student will listen and follow directions to make or do something.

Let's take a look at this timeless standard before we begin teaching and moving it into a Listening and Speaking station. Look closely at your own state standards for grade-level expectations and academic vocabulary. Students will first be exposed to listening and following directions to make or do something in whole group. After explicit instruction with engaging texts and tasks, they will then then be able to practice listening and following directions at the Listening and Speaking station independent of the teacher.

What It Is

- Following directions is being able to do what you are instructed to do, one step at a time, in a prescribed order to accomplish a task. Directions may be spoken and/or written.

- You may follow written directions to knit a scarf or draw a horse. You may follow directions to play a board game or a sport. Or you may follow directions to do something you must do as part of your job (e.g., fill out a form or report).

- Many YouTube tutorials are all about following directions!

Why It's Important

- Listening and following directions is important at school and in life! Some directions are given orally and must be followed for safety, such as fire drill procedures. Others streamline processes, such as directions for how to order and pick up food in the lunch line.

- Following instructions is critical when cooking a new recipe or learning a new sport or skill.

EL TIP: When working with multilingual students, it is critical to enunciate clearly, use gestures as needed, and give clear directions. Use familiar vocabulary when writing directions to help students be successful.

- Following directions on a test can make or break your score.

- There are many directions you must follow when using new technology. Teach kids how to follow directions, such as log-in procedures.

Myths and Confusions

- In some states, the standards for kindergarten and first grade require that children follow oral directions with multiple steps. I've found it most helpful to give just *one* direction at a time orally and have students do that, then give the next step. (And I've witnessed this with adults as well as children!) Ultimately, the important thing is to follow directions in order when there is a sequence to be followed.

- When there are multi-step directions, it may be helpful for these to be listed and followed, one at a time.

- Note that not all procedural text is written clearly! See Select Picture Books, Magazines, and Online Text in the next section for ideas on how to select the best text that will help kids follow directions.

Real-World Connections

- There are so many situations in real life where you must follow directions—driving a vehicle, boarding an airplane, signing in as a visitor to a school, checking out a book from the library, cooking a recipe, learning to play a new musical instrument or perform a new dance routine, executing a play in football, or using a new program online.

How Practice at the Listening and Speaking Station Helps Students

- Working with a partner at this station, children will have opportunities to listen and follow directions without the teacher having to be the one giving instructions.

- Children will be able to practice following directions with multiple steps in order to make or create something. They will have to pay attention to the order of the instructions to be successful.

- It's fun to create things with a partner while listening to directions. The focus is on listening comprehension, not reading comprehension at the Listening and Speaking station.

EL TIP: Give students who are new to this country experiences in which following directions helps them better understand the culture in which they're now living. You might ask them privately what they'd like to learn to do. Then incorporate that into listening and speaking lessons for your class.

EL TIP: When listening to follow directions, students have a chance to pause the recording and listen as often as needed. This repetition can help students with language learning, sentence structure, and conceptual understanding.

You will want to first model how to listen and follow directions in whole group multiple times until you observe that students are ready to do this with a partner at the Listening and Speaking station. It's important to teach children how to listen and follow step-by-step directions in order to create or do something before releasing them to try this on their own for additional practice at the Listening and Speaking station.

You may find that your state doesn't have an upper-grade standard that matches this one, but it is still an important skill for older students. Adapt the ideas in this section that work for you and your older kids. Ideas are included at the end of this section for converting the Listening and Speaking station into a Recording Studio station, which is especially popular with children in Grades 2–4.

Consider the following steps for whole group instruction to ensure student success with this standard:

1. Plan

Select Picture Books, Magazines, and Online Text

Because you'll be modeling the listening and speaking work students will eventually do in that station, think about this standard and the kinds of experiences and texts that will help children be successful with listening and following directions to make or do something.

Choose picture books and articles (print and online versions) that contain directions for things you know your students will be interested in making or doing (e.g., how to make slime). Ask for children's input. Be on the lookout for procedural text (a type of informational text).

You can often find directions for crafts or recipes in children's magazines. Or look online at sites like www.readinga-z.com that provide a wide variety of texts that can be downloaded by subscription.

Use the same types of recorded text at the Listening and Speaking station. You may need to record your own audio to go with the text you use, or have students do this at a Recording Studio. (Ideas for this can be found on page 154.)

Pick pieces with well-written step-by-step instructions for students to follow. Look for books and articles that meet the following criterion when selecting text for listening to and following directions:

EL TIP: Visuals are very important in helping multilingual students comprehend and learn new vocabulary. Be sure the texts they are listening to include illustrations or photographs to support following directions.

KINDERGARTEN	GRADES 1–2	GRADES 3–4
Simple step-by-step instructions Simple pictures/photos that accompany each step Numbered steps (e.g., 1, 2, 3) that make it easier for young children to follow Just one direction per page (if written in a book format) Materials that can be used by young children independently (e.g., craft sticks, precut pieces, glue stick, crayons)	Easy-to-follow directions with picture support for each step One to three numbered steps per page (if written in book format) A materials list with pictures at the beginning (It's easiest to make something if you have everything needed before you start.) Simple things kids can make or do without adult supervision	A materials list at the start A few pictures demonstrating the procedure to follow Time order words or numbers (e.g., *first*, *next*, *then* or 1. 2. 3.) Things eight- to ten-year-olds can do successfully (e.g., dance steps, art and crafts procedures, letter writing tips) You may find these on one page at the end of a nonfiction book

Find Technology to Encourage Following Directions

Technology is one way to add novelty to your lessons. As mentioned at the start of this section, there are many videos that require kids to follow directions while singing and dancing. Or, you can create your own.

Also, there are many YouTube videos that may be helpful in teaching how to do things your students may be interested in. These can be used in whole group and again at a Listening and Speaking station. Be sure to provide materials so students can actually perform the matching tasks. Paying attention and being successful will encourage them to follow directions.

2. Teach

Introduce Listening and Following Directions With Games

You might start teaching how to listen and follow directions using games. Online videos of songs like "Move and Freeze" are great for capturing young children's attention and engage them quickly and easily to pay attention and follow directions. "Simon Says" is another game where kids must follow oral directions, as is the classic "Red Light, Green Light."

EL TIP: Using video is one way to provide support for multilingual students who are learning to listen and follow directions. If students can hear *and* see a demonstration of how to do something, this may increase comprehension and vocabulary/language learning.

If you work with older students, create cards with individual directions on each, such as "Clap five times. Stomp your feet, one at a time, six times. Sing the alphabet song. Count by fives to fifty. Sit on the ground and say, I'm a great listener. Tweet like a bird three times. Moo like a cow two times. Hiss like a snake four times." Choose a card and have the class follow that direction read to them. Try reading two cards in a row and having students follow the directions in that order. Build up to four directions in a row. Kids might enjoy making their own cards to use in the game, too.

Following directions cards made by students.

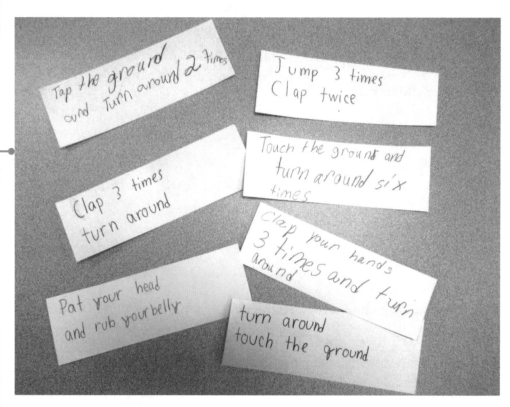

Use Read Aloud and Shared Reading to Help Students Follow Directions

After children show that they can listen to and follow oral directions, use read aloud or shared reading to teach how to follow directions to make or do something. Students will still be listening. But they will have the support of text and visuals to help them successfully follow directions. And if students get to make or do something, they will probably pay better attention to the directions.

I often use shared reading when working with procedural texts. Project directions for making or doing something on the board for the whole class to see. Choral read the text together (with the class as one voice) and think aloud about each step while students follow the directions.

Create Procedural Anchor Charts With Your Class

Make an anchor chart about following directions *with* your class. You might make simple charts on procedures you need kids to follow at school (e.g., what to do when I come to class; how to line up; how to walk in the hall; how to choose a book for independent reading). Be sure to add numbers for each step and photos for support.

Older students might make a video tutorial to accompany any of the above.

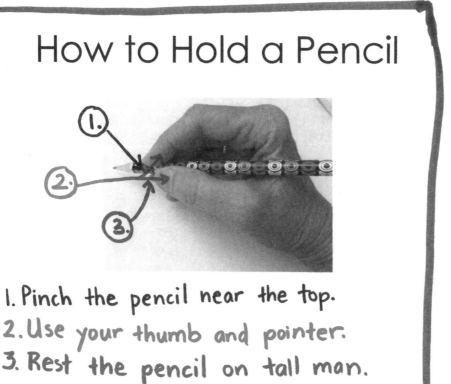

How to Hold a Pencil

1. Pinch the pencil near the top.
2. Use your thumb and pointer.
3. Rest the pencil on tall man.

Anchor chart made with the class about following directions to hold a pencil.

On the following pages are two lessons to use when teaching children about listening and following directions to make or do something. One could be used in kindergarten and Grade 1; the other is for Grades 2–4 and includes ideas for introducing a Recording Studio station. Please use these as samples to get you started with strong whole group lessons that will then be transferred to partner practice at the Listening and Speaking station.

SAMPLE LESSON for MODELING WITH A READ ALOUD BOOK in PRIMARY GRADES

MODEL TEXT: *How to Be a Cat* by Nikki McClure (a short book with directions to follow)

TIMELESS STANDARD: The student will **listen** and follow directions to make or do something. (Be sure this reflects your state and grade-level standards.)

VOCABULARY: *pounce, explore, tumble, stalk, feast*

TEACHER TALK:

- Listen for directions.
- Look at the pictures to help you follow directions.
- Follow directions in order.

STUDENT TALK: (Use matching printables on the companion website, **resources.corwin.com/simplystations-listening**. Kids will use these at the Listening and Speaking station, too.)

- I **hear** the **directions** _____. (Having students orally repeat directions will help them listen for specifics.)

LESSON STEPS:

The goal is for children eventually to understand how to listen and follow directions well enough that they can continue to do this without teacher assistance at the Listening and Speaking station. (Although this book isn't about a real-life thing to make or do, it's a simple playful text for demonstrating how to listen to and follow directions.)

1. Read aloud the title, *How to Be a Cat*, and tell students to listen for the directions the author gives us. Say: *The author tells us how to be a cat. Listen for her simple directions, one at a time.*

2. Read aloud the book, one page at a time, pausing to have young learners act out the page with you. For example, model how a cat would stretch and then have kids do this while repeating the word *stretch*.

3. Proceed with the rest of the book in the same way.

4. At the end of the book, review the directions the author gave for being a cat. Read the book again without showing the pictures this time. Have the students follow directions, page by page, in order.

EL TIP: Have multilingual students (as well as other class members) repeat a direction after it's heard. This can help them understand and develop new vocabulary/sentence structure.

5. On another day, reread the book to your class. Show the pictures and remind students to use the pictures to help them follow directions. Then read several pages of the book at a time without showing the pictures. Read two pages and see if kids can follow two directions in a row. If they can, try reading aloud three pages and have them follow three directions in a row.

QUICK ASSESS:

Did students follow directions, one at a time? How many simple directions can they follow in a row (up to three)?

AUTHOR'S CRAFT CONNECTION:

Help students closely examine the book they listened to. Again, the goal is for students eventually to talk about what authors do well enough that they can continue to have these discussions with a partner at the Listening and Speaking station (without the teacher being there). Author's Craft cards used during instruction and over time at a station will prompt students to do this without your help. (A matching printable can be found on the companion website, **resources.corwin.com/simplystations-listening**.)

With this read aloud book, students' talk might focus on how the author makes the pictures and words match. Also lead children to notice that most of the directions are action words—*stretch, clean, pounce.*

- How does the word match the picture on each page?
- Why do you think the author used the word _____ instead of _____ (e.g. *pounce* instead of *jump*)?
- Notice how the directions are in order. At the beginning of the book, it says stretch. At the end, it says dream. Why do you think the author did this? (A cat stretches when it wakes up; it dreams at the end of the day when it goes to sleep.)

EL TIP: Note that *brave* is not an action word. Remind students that we **can be** brave or *act* brave.

WRITING CONNECTION:

How to Be a Cat is a powerful text to use as a model for young writers learning to compose their own "how to" or procedural text. I like that the author only uses one word per page, which can make writing a less formidable task for children in kindergarten and early first grade. Help students brainstorm ideas for other how-to books that they may write (e.g., be a big brother or sister, go to school, walk down the hall). Then model how to write a book like this with your class. Sketch your picture and then work together to think of one action word that tells what to do. Write the word on the page, looking at *How to Be a Cat* for ideas on where to put the word on the page and what size to make the word.

Invite students to talk and write their own procedural text, thinking about what word to put on each page to give directions. Place this book at the Writing station after it's been used at the Listening and Speaking station for students to use as a model text for their own procedural text writing. Include "write a procedural book" as an option at the Writing station.

MOVING THIS LESSON TO PARTNER PRACTICE AT A STATION:

At the Listening and Speaking station, have kids work with a partner to listen to and follow directions using a recorded procedural text. Have them listen for directions, in order. Have one student be designated as the Pause Person who pushes the pause button to listen to a page or two, so they can then stop and follow those directions. (Be sure to model how to do this well! And if students are wearing headphones, teach them to remove these when following the directions.) You may make your own recordings for them to listen to with directions of things to do. See grade-level specific ideas at the end of this section.

One child is the Pause Person who pushes the pause button, so partners can stop to follow directions.

SAMPLE LESSON for MODELING WITH ONLINE SHARED READING in INTERMEDIATE GRADES

MODEL TEXT: *All About Kites* by Elizabeth Austin (from www .readinga-z.com and available at adjustable reading levels K, N, and R). I used Level R (third grade) for this lesson, so adjust vocabulary if you use a lower level.

TIMELESS STANDARD: The student will **listen** and follow directions to make or do something. (You might check your state standards related to reading and writing procedural text.)

VOCABULARY: *bridle* (this word is also in the book's glossary)

TEACHER TALK:

- This book includes procedural text. Listen for information about the topic and directions for how to do/make something.

- Listen carefully to each direction the author gives in procedural text that tells how to make or do something.

- Pay attention to the materials/ingredients needed in procedural text. It's usually written in a list.

- Stop and think about the steps to follow. An author writes these in order to help the reader be successful.

STUDENT TALK: (Use matching printable at **resources.corwin.com/ simplystations-listening**. Kids will use these at the Listening and Speaking station, too.)

- **Materials** needed for this **procedure** are _____. The author shows this by _____.

- The **author** shows us what to do in order by _____.

LESSON STEPS:

The goal is for students to eventually understand how to listen for and follow directions in order well enough so that they can continue to do this without teacher assistance at the Listening and Speaking station.

1. Project this book onto a screen and read the title with the class. Look at the table of contents and identify the genre (informational text).

2. Ask students which section might include procedural text or how to make or do something (*Make Your Own Kite*).

3. Page through the book with them, thinking aloud about what you'd find in each section.

4. Stop when you get to the last section, *Make Your Own Kite*. Have them tell how this text looks different from the rest of the book (e.g., *It has a list of what you'll need and step-by-step directions that are numbered.*)

5. Read this section with the students. Ask them what they'll need to make a kite.

6. On another day, gather materials (e.g., sticks, trash bags, cloth strips, tape, string, scissors) so there are enough for half the number of students in your class. (Kids will work with a partner, so you don't need materials for *each* student.)

7. Pair children at their tables or desks. Then read the materials list together, and have helpers distribute these. Ask students to check to be sure they have everything they need *before* following directions!

8. Then read the directions together, one step at a time, and have partners follow them to make a kite. Be sure kids get to fly their kites outdoors when weather permits!

9. End the lesson by asking students what they learned about listening to and following directions (e.g., *have all materials ready before attempting to make something, follow directions completely and in order*).

QUICK ASSESS:

Could students distinguish procedural text from other informational text? Did they follow directions in order?

AUTHOR'S CRAFT CONNECTION:

Looking at text through the lens of a writer can help students develop deeper comprehension and use some of these same techniques as they write. Use Author's Craft cards to help children closely examine how the author crafted this procedural text by using text features. (A matching printable can be found at **resources.corwin.com/ simplystations-listening**.) The goal is for learners to understand this well enough that they can do this without teacher assistance at the Listening and Speaking station. Here are some questions you might ask about author's craft of this text:

- Why did the author use a bulleted list at the beginning? (e.g., *to make the materials needed easier to read*; you need to get materials before you follow directions)

- How and where did the author use bold words? Why?

- Why do you think the author used dark black lines beside the directions? (e.g., *to see where a step started and ended*)

- Why did the author include illustrations to go with each step? What do you think would happen if there were no illustrations?

WRITING CONNECTION:

If you demonstrate how to write a procedural text using text features like lists, bold words, and illustrations, students will be more apt to do the same as they write at the Writing station. Model how to include these features as you write in front of your students. Encourage them to do the same as they write independently. Have them also read and try to follow directions their classmates have written.

MOVING THIS LESSON TO PARTNER PRACTICE AT A STATION:

At the Listening and Speaking station, have students work with a partner listening to and following directions together once they demonstrate understanding of how to do this using procedural text. Be sure to provide materials needed for them to make or do the simple things in the texts so they can follow the directions. You might also add the option of writing a how-to or procedural text at the Writing station once this has been taught well. Include samples of procedural texts, including some students have written, as models.

3. Partner Practice

Once you see that students are able to listen to and follow directions (that have been read aloud) with minimal teacher support, you're ready to move that same work into partner practice at the Listening and Speaking station. Expect learners to do what you've modeled well in whole group lessons.

Here are some additional, grade-level specific suggestions to help you think about meaningful work your students might do at the Listening and Speaking station as they focus on listening and following directions to make or do something:

Kindergarten

- Recorded directions for simple craft projects may be fun for students to follow at the Listening and Speaking station. Provide simple materials, such as precut paper shapes, crayons or markers, glue sticks, etc. (You may have to make your own recordings, or have students in an upper grade create these for you at a Recording Studio in their classroom.)

- Record directions, and number them one at a time, for kids to follow. (e.g., *1. Glue a yellow circle in the middle of your paper. 2. Color the top of your paper with a blue crayon. 3. Color the bottom of your paper with a green crayon. 4. Use a black crayon to draw a face on the yellow circle. 5. Draw something that makes you feel that way on the rest of your paper.*)

- Teach kids to listen to one direction and then pause the recording while they follow that step. Then listen to the next step and follow that direction.

- Look for little books for guided reading that can be recorded for kids to listen to and follow directions to make or do simple things.

- When they are finished listening, have partners turn and talk about what they made and the steps they took to make their picture. They might take a photo of their creation and share it with the class or family.

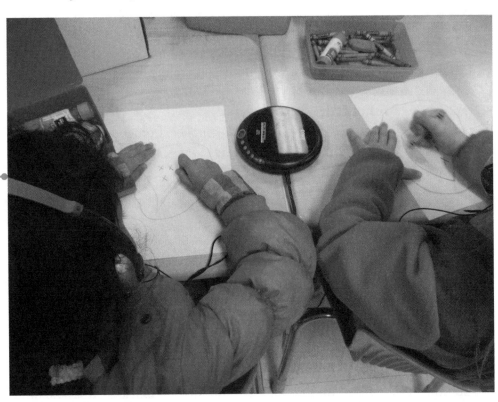

Students listen and follow directions to make a drawing at the Listening and Speaking station.

Grades 1–2

- Look for guided reading books with procedural text matching the reading levels of your students. Some publishers that offer high-quality procedural text books include Shell Education, Cherry Lake Publishing, Benchmark Education, and Capstone Press. You may need to make a recording to accompany the book if you can't find one already recorded. Or, ask strong readers to create these for you at a Recording Studio. (See directions in the Grades 3–4 ideas on the next page.)

- You might make your own recordings to go with procedural text found in magazines, such as *Ranger Rick*, *Highlights for Children*, and *Parents*.

- Provide all materials kids need to follow directions and successfully make what the book instructs them to do *with* a partner. They will need to pay attention to directions if they are to be successful! Plus, making stuff adds meaning to this station.

- Some students might want to make their own recordings (at a Recording Studio) with directions to follow. If they do, let them work with a partner to make a materials list and write directions before recording. (Check their work first to be sure others will be successful following these directions.)

- You might have one child listen to instructions and repeat back to their partner one step at a time. Also have them work together to follow the directions. This is a good way to incorporate listening *and* speaking into the station.

EL TIP: You might have multilingual students listen to a recording of a text with directions related to a concept for an upcoming science or social studies topic (e.g., how to read a map, how to use science equipment safely). This will familiarize them with new language and the concept. Sometimes children have conceptual understanding and just need the words to participate actively in a lesson.

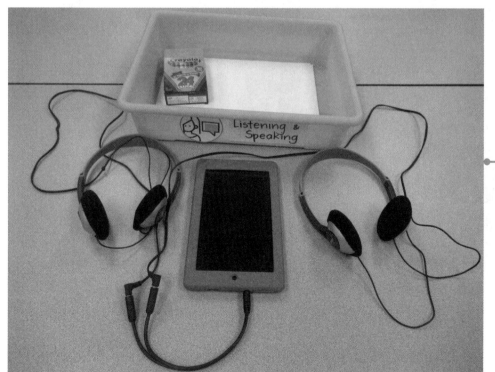

Materials organized for kids to use when following directions at a Listening and Speaking station.

EL TIP: Have students in upper grades who speak the same home language as your multilingual students create recordings in English for their schoolmates. Include the name and a photo of the student who made the recording. This enables newcomers to hear English read by others who have learned the language and provides an encouraging model.

- You might convert your Listening and Speaking station into a Recording Studio station. Or add the Recording Studio as a new station. Simply teach students how to record a text for others to listen to using an iPad or other device with a microphone. They might record a story for kids in a younger class. Or they may create recordings for their classmates on following directions from magazines that have one- or two-page pieces on how to make or do something. (Again, check out *Ranger Rick, National Geographic for Kids,* and *Highlights for Children* for great examples.) As students make recordings, remind them to pause after each direction to give listeners time to follow that step. Students can use the kid-friendly fluency tool available on the companion website, **resources.corwin.com/simplystations-listening**, for self-evaluation.

- Use online resources for step-by-step directions to follow. These often have voice recordings to accompany them. For instance, kids might watch videos that accompany the articles to make or do something with a partner. Again, emphasize listening *and* speaking. Have kids talk about what they made and the steps they followed after completing their craft or activity.

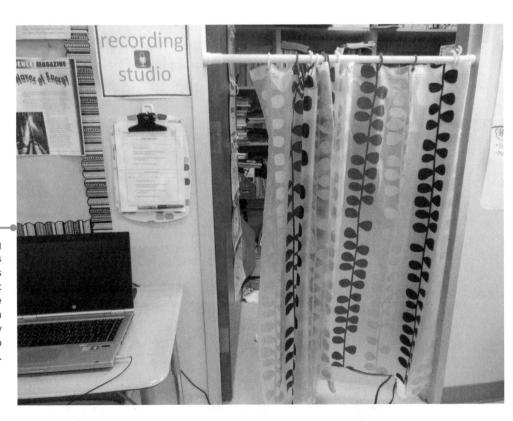

Space for a Recording Studio to record books for others to listen to is created with a transparent shower curtain (cut to the right height) mounted on a tension rod in a doorway of a classroom closet to create a quiet spot.

4. Reflect With Students

After your students have worked with this timeless standard at the Listening and Speaking station, reflect on what they've done here. Be sure to include a five- to ten-minute Reflection Time after stations where children can share what they learned to do or make at this station. Section 4 shows samples of forms you can download from the companion website, **resources.corwin .com/simplystations-listening**, to jot down your ideas about the work you and your children did. (There are matching printables at **resources.corwin .com/simplystations-listening** that you can also place at this station for readers to use while cleaning up.)

Here are some questions to use during Reflection Time regarding the Listening and Speaking station:

1. What did you make or do today as you followed directions at the Listening and Speaking station? (Students might show something they made to the class.)

2. What did the author do to help you follow directions?

3. Were you successful? Why or why not?

How-to book titled *How to Mix Colors*, written by a kindergartner at the Writing station.

Timeless Listening and Speaking Standard 5

The student will listen and take notes or share important information.

Let's take a look at this timeless standard before we begin teaching it in whole group and eventually moving it into a Listening and Speaking station. Look closely at your own state standards for grade-level expectations and academic vocabulary. Pay attention to standards related to research, gathering information, using sources, and determining importance. I've focused on listening to informational text in this section, but you could also apply this to listening to literary text.

What It Is

- Taking notes means to record the most important information in words and/or pictures.

- A picture is worth a thousand words! I've been learning to use a technique called Sketchnotes by designer Mark Rohde.

- While listening to information, we can jot down important and interesting facts to help us remember.

- We can talk with others about important and interesting information we've heard or learned by sharing our notes and findings. This is part of the research process, too.

Why It's Important

- When listening to news or informational text, listening for facts can help us determine what's most important. This can help us make sense of our world and learn new things.

- There is a lot of material included in informational text. If we can first listen and sift through it to determine importance, this will help us eventually do the same as independent readers.

- Learning to take notes on what we've heard precedes learning to take notes on what we've read. Jotting down important information can help us remember key ideas in informational text. Sharing those ideas is easier if we have notes to help us.

- Taking notes can help us focus and remember when listening and reading.

- Creating visual art can reduce stress, so taking notes through drawing can not only improve comprehension but may also reduce stress when students are listening and/or reading.

Myths and Confusions

- When asked to take notes or write what they've learned, children often want to copy what they've read word by word. Listening and discussing what's important can help students paraphrase or put what they've learned into their own words (orally at first and later in writing).

- Children listening to (or reading) informational text often think that everything is important. We can teach them how to listen for the most crucial information and record this in words or drawings.

- Some students will have difficulty writing words as they try to take notes. Model how to also use quick sketches to show comprehension of major events in stories and big ideas in informational text.

Real-World Connections

- When online, we are constantly barraged with information (news stories, video clips, ads). Learning to listen for what's important will help us make better decisions as consumers.

- When doing research, there is so much information to wade through in print and online. Learning to take notes/record important information helps us keep track of what we've learned and communicate this with others.

- I've learned to use Sketchnotes when taking notes at conferences. Instead of trying to write down everything the speaker says, I draw pictures to show big ideas which has freed me up to listen. It's also helped me to listen deeper. (Children can be taught to use Sketchnotes, too.)

EL TIP: Learning to take Sketchnotes greatly benefits multilingual students because of the visual nature of this note-taking system. Teach them to listen for big ideas and repeating concepts. Then show how to draw quick sketches to represent those ideas and connect the ideas with color, containers (e.g., boxes, circles, brackets), and arrows. Also show how to play with letters and fonts to emphasize big ideas.

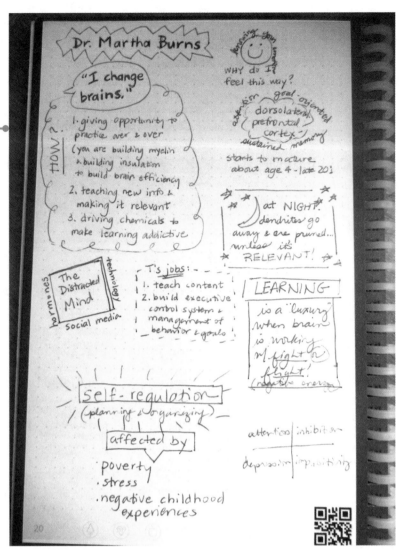

A sample of my own Sketchnotes from a conference.

How Practice at the Listening and Speaking Station Helps Students

- When students take notes while listening to recorded informational text at the Listening and Speaking station, it gives them opportunities to pay attention to the main ideas and supporting details.

- Working at this station gives children extra practice taking notes without the teacher having to lead instruction.

- Listening and then talking about text with a partner and taking notes gives learners the opportunity to deepen listening comprehension, which is the prerequisite for reading comprehension.

- Students with special education accommodations greatly benefit from working at the Listening and Speaking station. It familiarizes them with listening technology they may use when taking tests and may use in their jobs later in life.

It's important to teach concepts well in whole group before moving this work into the Listening and Speaking station. This will help students to eventually know how to practice the same activities with a partner independently of you. Consider the following steps for student success with this standard:

1. Plan

Select Picture Books, Magazines, and Online Text

Because you'll be modeling the listening and speaking work kids will do in the station, think about this standard and the kind of text that will help children understand the skill you're teaching. In this case, choose picture books and articles (print and online versions) that will pique student interest. Ask for children's input in what they'd like to learn about. This is a perfect place to tie in research and inquiry and answering questions using a variety of sources. Use the same types of recorded text at the Listening and Speaking station. Look for books and articles that meet the following criteria when selecting text for taking notes and sharing important information:

KINDERGARTEN	GRADES 1–2	GRADES 3–4
Simple familiar text and notes you've modeled with	Familiar text and notes you've modeled with	Texts related to inquiry questions your students have
Short text with strong picture support (just one or two lines of text per page)	Short texts related to inquiry questions your class has	Texts about science and social studies topics you are studying
Text about things four- and five-year-olds know about and are curious about (pets, families, toys)	Text with simple ideas from which first and second graders could jot down key ideas with words and sketches	Informational texts that students have recorded for others to listen to (and take notes)
Text with simple ideas that young children could draw/write about		

2. Teach

Model How to Take Notes

Model. Model. Model! Teaching students to take notes takes time and patience. You will need to model this process many times before releasing responsibility to children for doing this on their own at the Listening and Speaking station.

Use simple text with accompanying images and simple notes to begin. Think aloud as you take notes in front of students in whole group. It's helpful to show kids how to draw a quick sketch to help to remember important information, regardless of your artistic skill. The act of drawing helps your memory hold onto ideas! This may also help struggling writers take risks with note-taking.

Set Listening Goals

Tell students what you want them to listen for. Say, "Listen to find out _____." For example, "As you listen to *From Tadpole to Frog*, listen to find out the first step in a frog's life."

Or you might show the cover of an informational text called *Homes in Many Cultures* and read the table of contents to the students. Ask students what they should listen to find out based on the table of contents. Use the conversation card, *I will listen to find out* _____. (A printable can be found in at **resources.corwin.com/simplystations-listening**.)

Use an Anchor Chart to Teach How to Take Notes

Make an anchor chart on how to take notes *with* your class. List simple steps and label notes to show where they came from. Review these charts before reading aloud to help children focus their attention. Here are some sample charts for inspiration:

> **EL TIP:** Students comprehend better when they know *what* to listen for. Teaching multilingual students how to listen for and take notes on the most important ideas will help them tune into language and content.
>
> **EL TIP:** Visuals on your anchor charts will help all students, especially those who are learning a new language, better understand how to take notes.

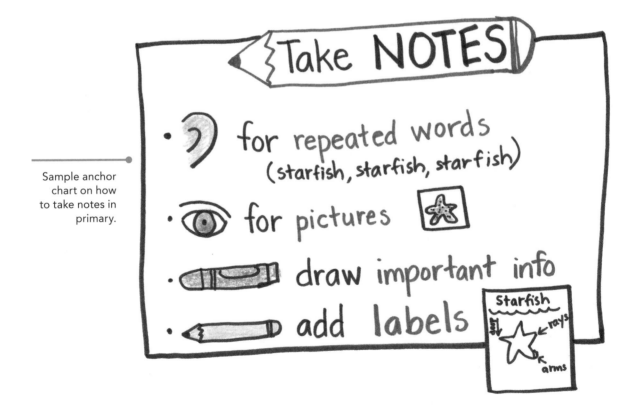

Sample anchor chart on how to take notes in primary.

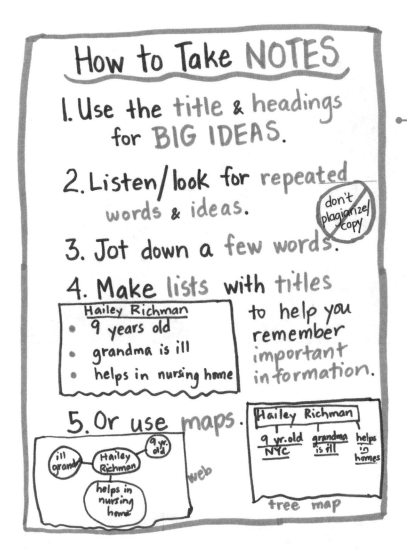

Another anchor chart on how to take notes in intermediate.

Listen, Then Jot

Show children how to listen to a section, talk to a partner, and then jot down something important. Model how you don't write everything you heard, just the important part. Teach them to listen to words that are repeated or things they didn't know before.

Use Graphic Organizers and Thinking Maps for Response/Remembering

Many teachers use graphic organizers to help their students organize their thinking and remember what they read or listened to. I like to also use Thinking Maps, a set of seven special thinking tools that can be used across disciplines. Visit www.thinkingmaps.com for ideas on how to incorporate these. Model well before asking students to use these at the Listening and Speaking station.

EL TIP: Listening to just a bit at a time will make comprehension less intimidating for multilingual students. Talking about what they've heard with a partner builds language and increases understanding. Working together to take notes builds confidence and skill.

Graphic organizers may be used at a Listening and Speaking station to help students take notes.

Use Sticky Notes to Remember Information

You might use sticky notes for recording information using sketches and words. Model how to jot one idea on each sticky note. Also show how to manipulate your sticky notes into categories to organize information learned, especially if students are doing research and using multiple sources.

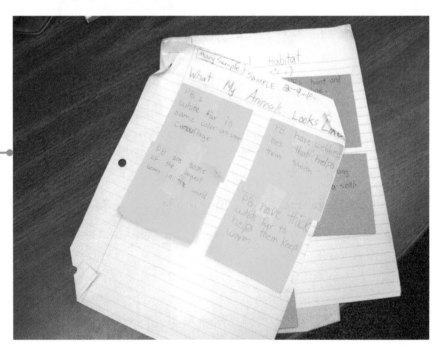

Sticky notes are organized to answer a research question.

On the following pages are two sample lessons for modeling to use when teaching children how to listen and take notes in whole group read aloud. One lesson is for primary grades and encourages them to draw pictures and use words, and the other is for Grades 2–4 and focuses more on written notes. Use these as examples to get you started with strong whole group lessons that will then be transferred to partner practice at the Listening and Speaking station. Please use titles that match the needs and interests of your students. I included sample texts for modeling and hope you'll repeat these lessons more than once with a variety of read alouds that introduce learners to a range of topics over time.

SAMPLE LESSON for MODELING WITH A READ ALOUD BOOK in PRIMARY GRADES

MODEL TEXT: *Starfish* by Edith Thacher Hurd (a short informational book with picture support)

TIMELESS STANDARD: The student will listen and take notes/share important information. (Tweak this, as needed, to match your state and grade-level standards.)

TEACHER TALK:

- Listen. Think about what you hear that's important.
- Listen. Sketch or quickly draw what you hear that's important.
- What do you hear that's interesting? Let's take a note on that.

STUDENT TALK: Use the conversation cards to demonstrate. (This printable is available at **resources.corwin.com/simplystations-listening**.) Kids will use these in whole group and over time at the Listening and Speaking station, too.

- I will **listen** to find out _____.
- An **important** thing I **heard** is _____.
- An **interesting** thing I **heard** is _____.

LESSON STEPS:

The goal is for students eventually to tell and then take notes on important or interesting information well enough in whole group, so they can continue to do this without teacher assistance at the Listening and Speaking station over time. This may take a lot of modeling, so be sure to repeat this lesson with a variety of informational texts.

1. Show the front cover and read the title. Have students turn and talk to a partner about what they see that's important or

interesting. Partner A tells Partner B. Then switch. Be sure to ask several students to share with the whole class what their partner said, using a sentence. For example, *The starfish is red. The starfish has five legs.* This encourages active listening and provides good models for speaking.

2. Tell students that you will teach them how to take notes to remember important information. Create or use an anchor chart on note-taking as you teach this lesson.

3. Quickly sketch a starfish using a thick black marker on white paper. And write *starfish,* too, since this is what you'll be taking notes on—the *topic* of the book.

4. Read aloud the first page and think aloud about important information. For example, *Starfish live in the sea. I'll sketch some waves to show the ocean. They live deep in the sea. I'll draw an arrow pointing down to show they are deep in the water.* Sketch and take notes in front of your class.

5. Repeat, reading aloud a page or two and adding important information to your notes. Use a combination of sketches and words, as shown in the photo.

6. Use your notes to review what was learned about starfish. Ask students to turn and talk again and then share what they learned using the notes.

7. On another day you might read another short text about starfish and have students point to information already in your notes. Take more notes as they hear additional important information.

Sample notes made with the class about the book *Starfish*.

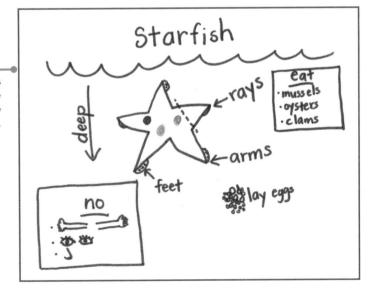

8. Over time, give partners a dry erase board and markers as you read aloud a short informational text and ask them to listen for important information. Read a bit, have them talk about what they heard, and then sketch it and hold up their boards for you to see.

QUICK ASSESS:

Did students tell important or interesting information they heard in the text? Are they listening or just looking at illustrations? (They should be doing both!) Did the information come from the words as well as the illustrations?

AUTHOR'S CRAFT CONNECTION:

Use Author's Craft cards to think about what the author did to help us pay attention to important information. (A matching printable can be found at the companion website, **resources.corwin.com/ simplystations-listening**.) The goal is for students to understand this well enough that they can eventually do this without teacher assistance at the Listening and Speaking station.

- What words did the author repeat? That can tell us what's important. (e.g., starfish, sea, arms, feet, rays, no, feet, clams)

- Look at the pictures. Find pictures that match the repeated or important words.

WRITING CONNECTION:

Teach students how to use notes to write something they learned. This will be helpful in science, math, or social studies, too. Think aloud as you model how to use notes and write sentences including that information. (*Starfish live in the sea. They have rays or arms. They use their feet to catch food like mussels, oysters, and clams. Starfish lay eggs which grow into adults.*)

MOVING THIS LESSON TO PARTNER PRACTICE AT A STATION:

At the Listening and Speaking station, have kids work with a partner using the same tools you used in whole group. Provide interesting short recorded text and dry erase materials. Remind them to listen, pause, talk, and take notes. Encourage them to use pictures and words. Don't expect young children to write summaries yet, but they might summarize what they learned by talking to one another using their notes.

EL TIP: Show a short video clip of real starfish to build background knowledge before or after reading aloud. Bring a starfish (shell) to class if you have one for kids to touch and talk about.

SAMPLE LESSON for MODELING WITH A READ ALOUD BOOK in INTERMEDIATE GRADES

MODEL TEXT: *Nine-Year-Old Girl Delivers Puzzles to Seniors with Alzheimer's Disease* by FamilyFun magazine, adapted by Newsela staff (https://newsela.com/read/elem-kid-volunteer) (set at Lexile level 680, fourth grade; reading levels can be adjusted up or down)

TIMELESS STANDARD: The student will listen and take notes/share important information. (Tweak this, as needed, to match your state and grade-level standards.)

TEACHER TALK:

- Listen for important information and jot it down in just a few words to take notes.

- What do you hear that's interesting? Write down a little bit to help you remember that information.

- You might use bullet points and make a list of what you hear. Or use sticky notes to jot down ideas.

- You might use a sketch and a few words to take notes. Focus on the most important ideas and ones that are repeated.

STUDENT TALK:

- An **important idea** I heard was _____.

- An **interesting idea** I heard was _____.

- I learned _____.

LESSON STEPS:

1. Project the online article onto the board and read the title and graphics with the class. Think aloud about the topic, Hailey Richman who helps people with Alzheimer's. Explain that Alzheimer's is a disease that makes older people forget things.

2. Write *Hailey Richman* at the top of a piece of paper or on the board and show how to take notes. Say, "I'm writing *Hailey Richman* and putting a box around it at the top of my notes, because she is who this article is about."

3. Read aloud a bit (the first few sentences) and pause. Think aloud about what's important information. Then jot down those ideas on a bulleted list or on individual sticky notes (e.g., nine years old,

lives in New York City, gives old people puzzles to help them). Explain that you're just writing down a few words with a bullet point in front to help you remember the most important ideas. (See a sample of notes made in list form with the class below.)

4. Then read aloud a few more sentences and model how to add a few more notes. Ask kids for their input.

5. You might also show learners how you could take notes using a sketch and a few words. (This is called Sketchnoting. See the example in the photo below.)

Sample notes made with the class about *Nine-Year-Old Girl Delivers Puzzles to Seniors with Alzheimer's Disease* in a bulleted list as well as in Sketchnote form.

EL TIP: You might show about thirty seconds of a video on kids talking to a woman with Alzheimer's to give background knowledge. A YouTube video is available, titled "Kids Meet a Woman with Alzheimer's" (uploaded by CUT; https://youtu.be/b9PhQ9yMu8Y). There's a particular snippet between time code 2:40–3:14 that shows how the woman forgets what she said, but the child shows empathy.

6. On another day, you might show a related video about Max Wallack, a seventeen-year-old who's designed puzzles to help seniors with Alzheimer's. Play the video and ask kids what they learned about Max. Then replay it, pausing it to jot down notes with important information about him. Model how to use Sketchnotes to record important ideas using pictures and words. (See a sample photo on the next page.)

7. After modeling several times, invite students to listen to another article of interest read aloud to them. Pause after every few sentences, have partners talk about important information they heard, and then have them work together to take notes in an interactive notebook or on a dry erase board. Model, model, model and give kids opportunities for supported practice in whole group before ever moving this work to the Listening and Speaking station.

(Max Wallack)
- Special puzzles for seniors — helps them feel successful & calm
- 17-year old designed them
- his great-grandma had Alzheimer's
- at age 12 founded "Puzzles to Remember" & got puzzle maker to make them (24,000+)
- wrote book for kids about Alzheimer's
- researches in college to prevent Alzheimer's
- wants to be a geriatric psychiatrist

These notes were made with the class while viewing a news clip on Max Wallack in both bulleted list and Sketchnote forms.

QUICK ASSESS:

Were students able to tell important or interesting information they heard in the article or video? Did they jot down just a few words (not a sentence) in a bulleted list or on sticky notes? Or did they use Sketchnotes? (One is not better than the other, they are just two different options to offer.) Did students connect ideas between texts and notice similarities from their notes?

AUTHOR'S CRAFT CONNECTION:

Use Author's Craft cards to think about what the author did to help us pay attention to important information. (A matching printable can be found at **resources.corwin.com/simplystations-listening**.) The goal is for students to understand this well enough that they can eventually do this without teacher assistance at the Listening and Speaking station.

- What words did the author repeat? That can tell us what's important. (e.g., Hailey, grandmother, Alzheimer's, charity, nursing home, puzzles)

- Why do you think the author chose these photographs? What important information do they show? (e.g., Hailey loves her grandma. Old people are doing easy puzzles. I think they may have Alzheimer's. Kids can help seniors.)

WRITING CONNECTION:

When you have finished taking notes, you might show students how to use your notes to write a summary of what you learned in the article. Have them help you as you write in front of them. (See the summary photo below, too.) If you used sticky notes, show kids how to move them around to organize notes that go together before writing.

If you show students how to use their notes to summarize what they heard, this can deepen comprehension. And over time they might do this at the Listening and Speaking station after they take notes with a partner, too. Use the notes you took to write summaries together in response to multiple read alouds before releasing this to students to do independently.

> Hailey Richman is a 9-year-old girl who lives in New York City and helps care for her grandma. Hailey's grandmother has Alzheimer's and has trouble remembering things, so she lives in a nursing home. Hailey has found ways to help seniors and kids. She takes puzzles to people with memory problems and runs KidCareGivers.com.

Sample summary written with the class
using notes on Hailey Richman.

MOVING THIS LESSON TO PARTNER PRACTICE AT A STATION:

At the Listening and Speaking station, have kids work with a partner using the same tools you used in whole group. Provide an interesting short recorded text and paper and pencil or dry erase materials. Remind them to listen, pause, talk, and take notes. Over time, you might also have students summarize what they heard using their notes to write a summary together.

3. Partner Practice

Once you see that students are able to listen and take notes in whole group, you're ready to move that same work into partner practice at the Listening and Speaking station. The goal is *not* for students to *just* use words for taking notes. Encourage kids to use drawings and words to show their thinking about big ideas in the text they listened to.

Here are some ideas of what children will be doing at the Listening and Speaking Station that move beyond just having students listen to a recorded book. Remember to first focus on having students listen actively and respond by talking about important information. Then move your attention to how to record those facts by drawing/writing notes. I've included additional grade-specific suggestions to help you think about the best things for your children to practice:

Kindergarten

- I'd start by having young children use familiar materials you've already taught with at the Listening and Speaking station. Have them listen to informational text previously read aloud. Include the notes you made in front of the class and ask partners to touch the corresponding notes as they listen.

- After listening, have partners work together to retell what they listened to, using the notes included.

- Over time, provide a large dry erase board where students may jot down notes as they listen to new informational text. Their notes will probably be drawings. Look for labels and words jotted down to represent facts.

Young learners work together to write (pictorial) notes on a dry erase board in response to what they heard at the Listening and Speaking station.

Grades 1–2

- Learning to take notes will take a lot of practice. Again, start by having students use materials at the Listening and Speaking station you've already taught with. Have kids listen to familiar informational text. Include the notes you made as a class for them to point to as they listen.

- After listening, have partners work together to retell what they listened to, using the notes included.

- Over time, provide a place (like an interactive notebook or dry erase materials) where children can record notes about important information from the text they listened to. Remind them to listen, pause, talk, and take notes. They might take their own notes and compare these with their partner's notes. Allow them to use sketches and words in their notes.

- If your students are engaged in inquiry or research, include recorded text that will help to answer their questions.

- You might substitute videos for recorded text for kids to listen to and take notes. Model how to pause the video (just like they did with recorded books) to help them pay attention and take notes.

Students listen to familiar text and point to notes made as a class to learn more about note taking.

Grades 3–4

- Students at these grade levels should get in the habit of writing notes with paper and pencil or capturing them on a device. Remind learners to listen to just a bit and then jot down notes. They may pause the recording as they listen and write things down.

- Provide blank sticky notes at the Listening and Speaking station for kids to use as they listen to recorded books. Have them jot down important information on sticky notes and organize these with their partner after listening. Encourage children to talk about what they learned, using their notes.

- Have upper-grade kids listen to podcasts and take notes. Then they can talk with a partner about what they visualized or learned. See Section 4 for recommended podcasts to use at the Listening and Speaking station.

- Students might listen to recorded information related to research and inquiry projects. Taking notes on sticky notes will allow them to manipulate these to organize information later. Teach them how to note sources, too. They might use a different colored sticky note for each source they use.

- If you have kids that simply copy the text, you might choose to not include printed copies and have them just focus on listening.

Older students use a tree map (thinking map) to take notes while viewing and listening to a video clip on glaciers.

- Substituting short video clips for kids to listen to and take notes works for older kids, too. Model how to pause the video (just like they did with recorded books) to help them pay attention and take notes. Use clips related to what students are learning about in content areas to help build background knowledge.

4. Reflect With Students

After your students have worked with this timeless standard at the Listening and Speaking station, reflect on what they've done here. Be sure to include a five- to ten-minute Reflection Time after stations where children can share important information with others about what they learned using the drawings/written notes they took at this station. Section 4 of this book shows samples of forms you can download from the companion website, **resources.corwin .com/simplystations-listening**, to jot down your ideas about the work you and your children did.

Children may use the questions below to talk about the work they did at the Listening and Speaking station related to taking notes. Older students might use the printable reflection questions available on the companion website, **resources .corwin.com/simplystations-listening**, to discuss what they learned as they clean up. Use these questions with the class during Reflection Time, too:

1. Tell some important information you heard in the book or video you listened to at this station today.

2. Share the notes you and your partner took at the station today. What's something interesting you found out?

3. If you wrote a summary at the Listening and Speaking station today, please read it to the class.

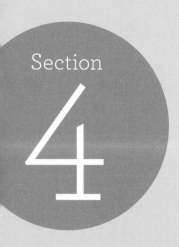

Reflection, Printables, and Resources

iStock.com/PeopleImages

This section is designed to provide everything you need to keep the Listening and Speaking station strong as your students grow more independent throughout the school year. It starts with questions to use for personal **reflection**, things to discuss in Professional Learning Community (PLC) or data team meetings with your grade level, and questions for students to use when thinking about their work at this station.

Next you'll find an introduction to the **printable** tools available on the companion website, **resources.corwin .com/simplystations-listening**, to help you get started with stations: icons for the management board and matching signs; planning calendars to use when introducing and rolling out stations; a checklist of routines to model for the Listening and Speaking station; and a chart for the Listening and Speaking Operations Test. Also included are

resources.corwin.com/
simplystations-listening

printable pages that match Sample Lessons for Modeling and suggestions from Section 3 of this book. You will find a blank conversation card template to personalize and make your own, based on your state standards and academic vocabulary. These printables are available online in English and Spanish.

Finally, in this section I've provided **resources** for materials you might use at the Listening and Speaking station, including sources for recorded books and a bibliography of all the books used in the lessons in Section 3.

I'd love to hear from you about sources you use for this station, too. Please use the hashtag #simplystations on social media. You can find me online at the following:

#simplystations

@debbie.diller (Instagram)

dillerdebbie (Facebook)

@debbiediller (Twitter)

www.debbiediller.com (website)

Reflection Tools

After your students have been working at the Listening and Speaking station for a while, here are some questions to reflect on throughout the school year. Use the Teacher Reflection Questions and PLC Reflection Questions on the companion website, **resources.corwin.com/simplystations-listening**, to record what you've tried, what's worked, and what you might change in the future. I recommend making several copies of these reflection sheets and filling them in at the beginning, middle, and end of the school year, or at the end of each term.

Teacher Reflection

1. Use this rubric to evaluate how this station is working after you introduce it. On a scale of 1–5, how did your Listening and Speaking station work?

Where I placed it in the classroom			
Ease of introducing routines			
Kids' operation of equipment			
	1	**2**	**3**

Not Well

2. Based on your ratings above, what could you do differently to improve how

3. Observe students in this station. What do they spend most of their time do most engaged? Least?

4. Compare students' listening to their speaking opportunities at this station Listening? Speaking? Good mix of both?

5. Think about the types of text students listened to at the Listening and Spe of texts were fiction? Nonfiction? What do your students need the most exp comprehension?

6. Which of the lessons from Section 3 did you try? What did your students le the Listening and Speaking station?

PLC Reflection

1. As a team, look at student data across your grade level. In what areas do children need more instruction? More practice?

2. Which of your students could benefit from more time at a Listening and Speaking station? How could this help them?

3. What's gone well at your Listening and Speaking station? Why?

4. What will you change at the Listening and Speaking station based on your discussion?

5. Compare the Listening and Speaking station for primary and intermediate students. What do you see that's the same for both? What's different? What benefits are there regardless of grade level?

Student Reflection Cards

I recommend that you save five to ten minutes each day for Reflection Time after stations and small group time. Gather your students to the whole group meeting area and talk with them about a few stations they worked at that day. This will provide what I call "paperless accountability" and lets kids know you care about what they practiced and learned today. It also will help you troubleshoot and provide ongoing positive reminders about what to do at stations. You won't have time to ask kids about every station every day. So choose just one or two stations to reflect on each day.

On the companion website, you'll find a set of printable reflection cards to use *following* stations and small group to discuss the Listening and Speaking station. Each matches a timeless standard for listening and speaking from Section 3. I've labeled them for ease of use: Timeless Standard 1 is TS1, and so on.

TIME-SAVING TIP: Print all the reflection cards for the Listening and Speaking station on cardstock. Hole-punch them in the upper left-hand corner and place them on a 1" book ring for ease of use. Keep them in your whole group teaching area for quick reference.

HOW to USE REFLECTION CARDS

1. Gather your class to the carpet following stations and small group time for Reflection Time.

2. Choose a few stations to discuss.

3. Use a reflection card to match what kids have been practicing at that station.

4. Ask one or two questions from the card.

5. Repeat with a reflection card to match practice at another station.

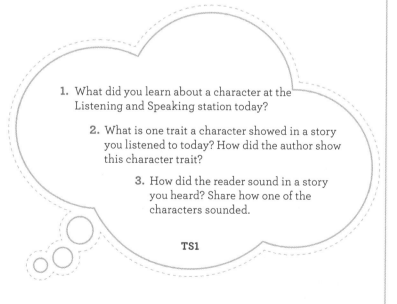

1. What did you learn about a character at the Listening and Speaking station today?

2. What is one trait a character showed in a story you listened to today? How did the author show this character trait?

3. How did the reader sound in a story you heard? Share how one of the characters sounded.

TS1

Fluency Reflection Tool

Here is a kid-friendly fluency reflection tool you might teach students to use at the Recording Studio station. To teach the class how to use this tool, I like to first project the form on the board and tell kids what to pay attention to (punctuation, phrases, interesting voices, different character voices) as I point to that part of the sheet. Then I read aloud a short selection from a familiar text and have students fill out the fluency reflection tool with me. I think aloud about how I'm scoring myself and why. Talk with students about what to do differently to improve fluency on the next read. You might also work with students in small group to be sure they know how to use the fluency reflection tool before moving it to the Recording Studio station for kids to use independently.

[How Fluent Was My Reading?]

Name _____ Date _____

Record your reading. Then listen to your recording and answer these questions.

	NO	SOMETIMES	YES
1. Did I stop at punctuation?			
2. Did I read smoothly in phrases?			
3. Did I sound interesting?			
4. Did my voice sound like different characters?			

To improve my fluency I will …

Planning Tools

As noted in Section 2, using a roll-out calendar helps in plotting out when you'll introduce each station throughout the first few weeks of school helps smooth implementation. Also plan for a "reboot" periodically where you'll commit to looking closer at what students are doing at that station. Be ready to add/change/replace things at that time. The companion website includes blank forms you can use for planning stations roll-out and refresh. See pages 15–16 for a sample filled-in calendar. Remember to recycle things from whole group into stations, so you can work smarter, not harder.

TIME-SAVING TIP: Make a master calendar to plan for when you'll introduce and reboot each station. If you have others on your grade level, plan and work together to simplify the roll-out of each station.

Roll-Out Calendar

for Introducing and Refreshing Stations

AUGUST		SEPTEMBER	
Week 1		Week 1	
Week 2		Week 2	
Week 3		Week 3	
Week 4		Week 4	

OCTOBER		NOVEMBER	
Week 1		Week 1	
Week 2		Week 2	
Week 3		Week 3	
Week 4		Week 4	

Use the Checklist of Routines to help you remember to model everything needed for children to be successful at the Listening and Speaking station. There's a space to jot notes and reflect on how your launch lessons went for future reference.

Use the Simply Stations Planning Tool when planning instruction from standards to stations. I recommend working with a team to do this. Also see Section 3, pages 44–45, for suggestions for using this tool individually or with your team.

The Chart for Passing the Operating Test can help you keep track of who knows how to correctly operate the listening equipment. Use for students who might need a little extra help to be sure they know how to use the Listening and Speaking station before sending them there.

Download blank, printable planning tools from the companion website, **resources.corwin.com/simplystations-listening.**

[**Checklist of Routines**]

to Model and Expect at the Listening and Speaking Station

Use this checklist to help you remember to model everything needed for children to be successful at the Listening and Speaking station. There's a space to jot notes and reflect on how your launch lessons went for future reference.

Listening and Speaking Station Routines: MODEL HOW TO …

ROUTINE MODELED	DATE INTRODUCED	MY NOTES
Use listening equipment (devices and splitter)		
Use and put headsets/earbuds away neatly		
Take materials to a designated spot in the classroom		
Find a book to listen to quickly and easily		
Share a book by having each child hold one side of the book while listening		
Pause/stop a recording and remove headsets/earbuds to talk to a partner		
Respond with a partner by talking, drawing, writing, etc.		
Clean up materials neatly at the end of stations time		

Simply Stations Planning Tool

STANDARD WE'RE TEACHING	ACADEMIC VOCABULARY	WHOLE GROUP IDEAS	PARTNER PRACTICE AT LITERACY STATIONS
			_____ Station
			→

Chart for Passing the Operating Test

at the Listening and Speaking Station

Place an X in each box to show the child can do this task before allowing students to work with a partner at the Listening and Speaking station. Refer to this list as needed to remind specific students that they know what to do and have already proven this.

CHILD'S NAME AND DATE	FIND BOOK TO LISTEN TO Child can quickly find recording to listen to.	HEADSET USE Child can plug in headset and put it away neatly.	SPLITTER USE Child can plug in splitter tightly and hear recording.	PLAY, PAUSE, AND STOP Child can turn device on and off alone.	TALK WITH CORRECT VOICE LEVEL Child can talk at a quiet voice level with a partner.	CLEAN UP Child can return all materials neatly to the bin.

Icons *and* Signs

The companion website, **resources.corwin.com/simplystations-listening**, includes printable icon cards for your management board and full-page foldable signs for each station. You can use these icons as matching signs to label spaces around the room where students will work at literacy stations. This will help learners know where to go quickly and easily.

Listening and Speaking Station

Independent Reading Station

Partner Reading Station

Writing Station

Poetry Station

Drama Station

Word Study Station

Inquiry and Research Station

Let's Talk Station

Recording Studio

Meet With Teacher

Printable Tools *for* Teaching *and* Transfer

The companion website, **resources.corwin.com/simplystations-listening**, contains many full-page printables for teachers to use in whole-group lessons and for students to use in stations. In this section, you'll find a visual index of what's available online, with any relevant notes or instructions for use.

All printables correspond to the Timeless Standards lessons in Section 3 of this book. Use them when teaching in whole and small group, where appropriate. Then transfer them to the Listening and Speaking station. The reproducibles are organized by Timeless Listening and Speaking Standard to make them easy to find.

You'll find all of these items in full-page printable format online:

Timeless Listening and Speaking Standard 1
Character Traits List: Grades K–1, Grades 2–4
Graphic Organizers: Circle Map, Character Feelings Chart, Thinking About a Character
Conversation Cards for Describing and Discussing Characters: Grades K–1, Grades 2–4
Author's Craft Cards for Describing and Discussing Characters: Grades K–1, Grades 2–4

Timeless Listening and Speaking Standard 2
Conversation Cards for Asking and Answering Questions: Grades K–1, Grades 2–4
Author's Craft Cards for Asking and Answering Questions: Grades K–1, Grades 2–4

Timeless Listening and Speaking Standard 3
Graphic Organizers: Multiple Meaning Words, New Words, Frayer Model
Conversation Cards for Listening to and Using New Vocabulary: Grades K–1, Grades 2–4
Author's Craft Cards for Listening to and Using New Vocabulary: Grades K–1, Grades 2–4

Timeless Listening and Speaking Standard 4
Conversation Cards for Following Directions: Grades K–1, Grades 2–4
Author's Craft Cards for Following Directions: Grades K–1, Grades 2–4

Timeless Listening and Speaking Standard 5
Conversation Cards for Listening and Taking Notes: Grades K–1, Grades 2–4
Author's Craft Cards for Listening and Taking Notes: Grades K–1, Grades 2–4

Conversation Cards

for Describing and Discussing Characters

The companion website, **resources.corwin.com/simplystations-listening**, contains larger printables of every conversation card to use in each of the Timeless Standards lessons and at stations when children practice the skills. Model how to use these cards in whole group before ever moving them into the Listening and Speaking station. Remember, you can modify these cards according to your students' needs and your standards.

GRADES K–1 CONVERSATION CARD EXAMPLE

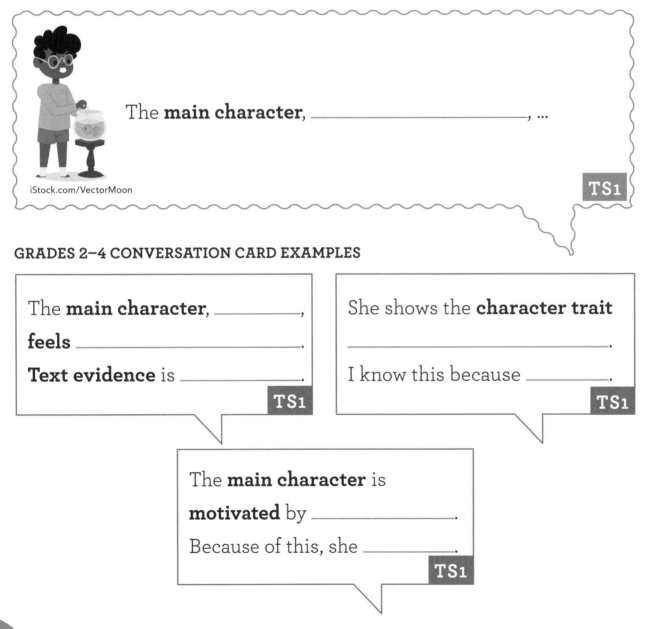

The **main character**, _____, ...

iStock.com/VectorMoon

TS1

GRADES 2–4 CONVERSATION CARD EXAMPLES

The **main character**, _____,
feels _____.
Text evidence is _____.

TS1

She shows the **character trait**
_____.
I know this because _____.

TS1

The **main character** is
motivated by _____.
Because of this, she _____.

TS1

Conversation Cards

for Asking and Answering Questions

The companion website, **resources.corwin.com/simplystations-listening**, contains larger printables of every conversation card to use in each of the Timeless Standards lessons and at stations when children practice the skills. Model how to use these cards in whole group before ever moving them into the Listening and Speaking station. Remember, you can modify these cards according to your students' needs and your standards. You'll notice that these cards are connected to promote asking and answering.

GRADES K–1 CONNECTED CONVERSATION CARD EXAMPLE

GRADES 2–4 CONNECTED CONVERSATION CARD EXAMPLE

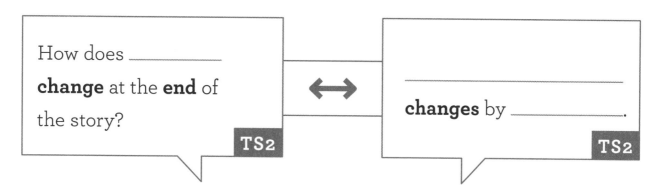

GRADES K–1 CONVERSATION CARD EXAMPLE

My **question** is _____

_____ .

TS2

GRADES 2–4 CONVERSATION CARD EXAMPLES

To **listen actively**, I _____

_____ .

TS2

My **question** is _____

_____ .

TS2

I'm not sure about _____

_____ .

TS2

Conversation Cards

for Listening to and Using New Vocabulary

The companion website, **resources.corwin.com/simplystations-listening**, contains larger printables of every conversation card to use in each of the Timeless Standards lessons and at stations when children practice the skills. Model how to use these cards in whole group before ever moving them into the Listening and Speaking station. Remember, you can modify these cards according to your students' needs and your standards.

GRADES K–1 CONVERSATION CARD EXAMPLE

My **new word** is _____.

It **means** _____.

I know this because _____.

iStock.com/Vectorios2016

TS3

GRADES 2–4 CONVERSATION CARD EXAMPLES

_____ is a **multiple-meaning word**.

It means _____ here.

It can also mean _____.

TS3

A **new meaning** for _____ is _____.

Another definition for this word is _____.

TS3

Conversation Cards

for Following Directions

The companion website, **resources.corwin.com/simplystations-listening**, contains larger printables of every conversation card to use in each of the Timeless Standards lessons and at stations when children practice the skills. Model how to use these cards in whole group before ever moving them into the Listening and Speaking station. Remember, you can modify these cards according to your students' needs and your standards.

GRADES K–1 CONVERSATION CARD EXAMPLE

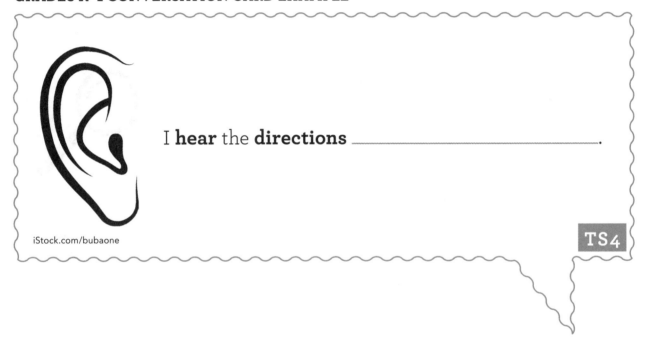

I **hear** the **directions** _____.

iStock.com/bubaone

TS4

GRADES 2–4 CONVERSATION CARD EXAMPLES

Materials needed for this **procedure** are _____.

The **author** shows this by _____.

TS4

The **author** shows us what to do in order by _____.

TS4

Conversation Cards

The companion website, **resources.corwin.com/simplystations-listening**, contains larger printables of every conversation card to use in each of the Timeless Standards lessons and at stations when children practice the skills. Model how to use these cards in whole group before ever moving them into the Listening and Speaking station. Remember, you can modify these cards according to your students' needs and your standards.

GRADES K–1 CONVERSATION CARD EXAMPLE

I will **listen** to find out _____.

iStock.com/bubaone

TS5

GRADES 2–4 CONVERSATION CARD EXAMPLES

An **important idea** I heard was _____.

TS5

An **interesting idea** I heard was _____.

TS5

Author's Craft Cards

The companion website, **resources.corwin.com/simplystations-listening**, contains larger printables of every author's craft card to use in each of the Timeless Standards lessons and at stations when children practice the skills.

GRADES K–1 AUTHOR'S CRAFT CARD EXAMPLES

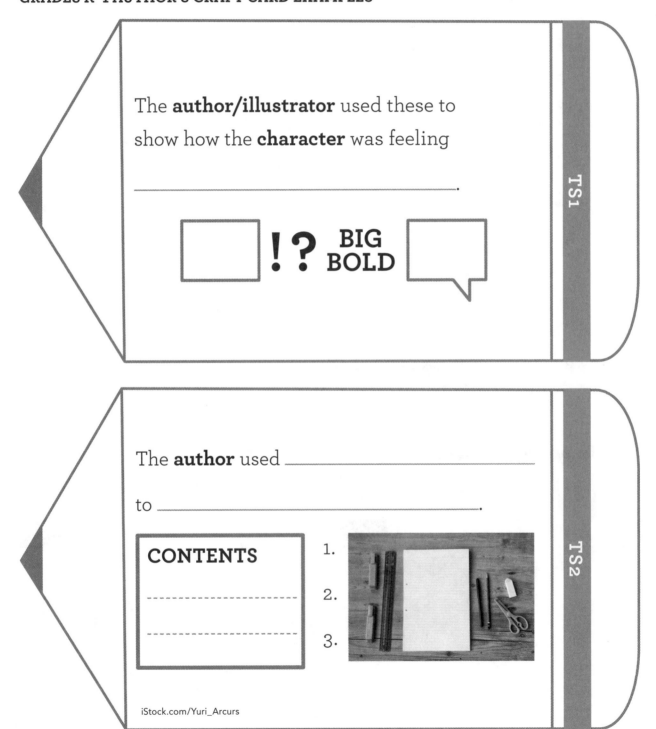

The **author/illustrator** used these to show how the **character** was feeling

_____.

▢ **!?** **BIG BOLD** 💬

TS1

The **author** used _____

to _____.

CONTENTS
- - - - - - - - - - - -
- - - - - - - - - - - -

1.
2.
3.

TS2

iStock.com/Yuri_Arcurs

- How did the **author** tell the **reader** what the **main character** was feeling?

- How did the **illustrator** show the **main character's** feelings?

- Look at the **author's** use of **conversation** in this story. Why do you think the **author** used so much **dialogue**? Was the whole story written in **dialogue**? Why not?

- Examine the **author's** use of *italics* in this **story**. Why do you think the **author** *italicized* those particular words?

TS1

- What got your attention in this book? What helped you to **listen actively**?

- How did the **authors** use **questions** in this book? Why do you think they used a **question** where they did?

- How is this **story** like another story you have read? When and how did you figure that out?

- Examine the **authors' use of color** in this book. Why do you think they did this?

TS2

Graphic Organizers

The companion website, **resources.corwin.com/simplystations-listening**, contains full-size printables of every graphic organizer to use in each of the Timeless Standards lessons and at stations when children practice the skills.

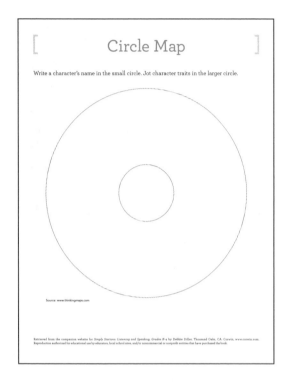

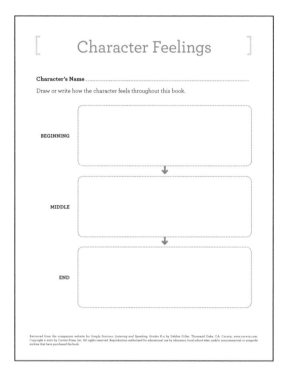

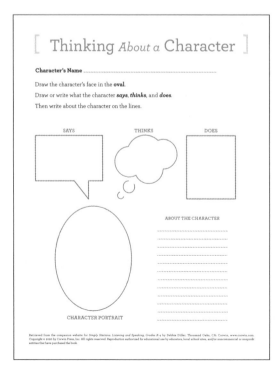

[Multiple Meaning Words]

Listen for multiple meaning words.

Write a word in each space and draw a picture to show its meaning. Show all the other meanings you know, too.

<table>
<tr><td></td><td></td><td></td></tr>
<tr><td></td><td></td><td></td></tr>
<tr><td></td><td></td><td></td></tr>
</table>

[New Words]

Listen for new words.

Write a new word in each box.

Draw a picture to match the word.

[Frayer Model]

Write the new word in the circle. Then fill in the boxes.

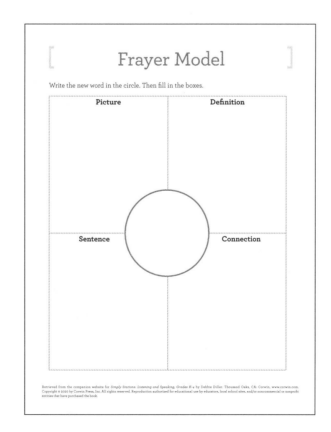

Recording Studio Station Ideas

You may want to teach students how to make a recording of a favorite book for others to listen to at the Listening and Speaking station. You might even rename it Recording Studio station. Teach kids how to follow directions to record. Here is a sample you might use. Model well before releasing partners to do this independently!

HOW TO RECORD A BOOK (for OTHERS to LISTEN to)

1. Practice reading the book several times, so you sound interesting.

2. Have your device and book ready. You might want a bell to signal when to turn the pages.

3. Read into the recorder with a clear voice. Be sure you have pushed "Record."

4. Make your voice sound like the characters.

5. When you are finished recording, listen and then save it.

Resources

You will want students to listen to a variety of recorded texts at the Listening and Speaking station throughout the year. Change out what they listen to periodically. And remember it's okay to have children listen to the same text more than once. You don't have to change out the Listening and Speaking station every week! Also, give kids a choice of what to listen to. You might provide three to five selections at a time.

Teachers often ask me where to find things for students to listen to at the Listening and Speaking station. I've listed resources below that have been tested and approved by me and a number of other teachers over the years. Choose those that best match what you're teaching and your students' needs.

Free Stuff to Listen to

These are recorded book sources that can be downloaded or played via CD, MP3 file, iTunes, or in the Google Play store:

- **http://www.openculture.com/freeaudiobooks** – 1,000 audiobooks from Aesop's fables to *The Secret Garden*

- **https://www.learnoutloud.com/Kids-Audio-Books** – over 150 titles including books by Roald Dahl and C.S. Lewis, as well as Sesame Street podcasts

- **https://www.storynory.com** – fairytales, myths, and legends recorded in Great Britain

- **https://etc.usf.edu/lit2go** – more than 1,000 recordings that can be searched by author, title, genre, or readability level ranging from kindergarten through high school

- **http://www.gutenberg.org** – over 58,000 e-books that have free access in the United States

- **https://openlibrary.org** – e-books for kids and adults you can loan for free

- **http://en.childrenslibrary.org** – many stories from all over the world

- **https://www.overdrive.com** – used by many public libraries (You can access it for free if you have a public library card.)

- **https://www.hoopladigital.com** – free with many public library services

- **www.bookshare.org** – free for children with a qualifying disability, such as dyslexia (see the site for more details)

- **https://librivox.org** – free public domain literature read by volunteers from around the world

- **http://www.loyalbooks.com** – free public domain books

Or try podcasts for your upper-grade students to listen to. Here are a few to get you started:

- *The Adventures of Eleanor Amplified* – from PBS, a radio reporter, Eleanor, outsmarts villains and teaches life lessons (**https://whyy.org/programs/eleanor-amplified**)

- *The Radio Adventures of Dr. Floyd* – a show about a scientist who fights his arch enemy, Dr. Steve, that teaches about the history of the earth (**http://www.doctorfloyd.com**)

- *The Show about Science* – a radio show for kids who are curious about science (**https://theshowaboutscience.com**)

- *Tumble* – a science series that answers kids' questions and tells stories about science discoveries (**http://www.sciencepodcastforkids.com**)

Subscription Sources for Recorded Books

The following recorded book sources are available through a subscription service. Check with your school system. You may already have access!

- Epic!

- myON

- Tumblebooks

- Spotify

- Audible

- Simply Audiobooks

- Learning Ally Audio

- Downpour

- Tales2go

- ReadingIQ

Other Places to Find Recorded Books

- Live Oak Media produces high-quality CDs and sells matching children's books. They also sell audiobooks. Their read-alongs are available for streaming, too. Go to **www.liveoakmedia.com** for more information.

- Weston Woods Studios produces amazing animations of children's books. They have many English titles, some in Spanish, and even have related author interviews. Check them out at **www.westonwoods .scholastic.com**.

- BookFlix is another source for excellent animated recorded books for Grades K–3. This subscription service from Scholastic pairs classic fiction and nonfiction titles on the same topic. Books are read by celebrity voice actors and the animation makes titles come alive!

- TrueFlix, another subscription service from Scholastic, is a multimedia resource for Grades 3–6 that provides support for learning social studies and science concepts. It includes introductory videos to build background knowledge, e-books, and a read aloud component, so children can use this at a Listening and Speaking station.

- Check with your school and public libraries for recorded books. They may have CDs and matching books for you to borrow. Today you can get almost anything on interlibrary loan!

- Try garage sales and online auctions like eBay to find inexpensive CDs and matching books, too.

- Join a local group on www.freecycle.org and ask for books and matching CDs for kids.

- Write a mini grant for things for your students to listen to. Sites like www.donorschoose.org and www.adoptaclassroom.org are fast and easy to use.

- Contact curation specialists like **http://www.stepstoliteracy.com/** to create a customized listening library for your classroom or school.

BIBLIOGRAPHY of TEXTS USED in LESSONS

TEXT USED IN SAMPLE MODEL LESSONS	STANDARD AND GRADE LEVELS	PAGE NUMBER FOR THE LESSON
Austin, E. (2003). *All about kites*. Retrieved from www.readinga-z.com.	TS4 Intermediate	109
Bunting, E. (1998). *Going home*. New York, NY: HarperCollins.	TS3 Intermediate	93
Choi, Y. (2003). *The name jar*. New York, NY: Penguin Books.	TS1 Intermediate	60
Newsela staff (2017, May). Nine-year-old girl delivers puzzles to seniors with Alzheimer's disease. Adapted from *FamilyFun*.	TS5 Intermediate	126
Hurd, E. T. (2000). *Starfish*. New York, NY: HarperCollins.	TS5 Primary	123
McClure, N. (2013). *How to be a cat*. New York, NY: Abrams.	TS4 Primary	106
Shores, E. L. (2011). *How to make bubbles*. Mankato, MN: Capstone Press.	TS2 Primary	73
Stevens, J., & Crummel, S. S. (2011). *The little red pen*. New York, NY: HMH Books for Young Readers.	TS2 Intermediate	75
Willems, M. (2010). *City dog, country frog*. New York, NY: Hyperion.	TS3 Primary	90
Willems, M. (2004). *The pigeon finds a hot dog*. New York, NY: Hyperion.	TS1 Primary	58

 **Because...**
ALL TEACHERS ARE LEADERS

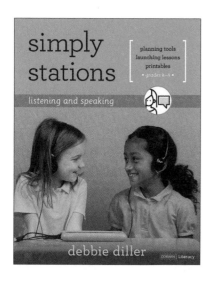

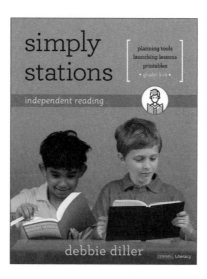

Debbie Diller has been refining literacy stations for over 40 years, working with thousands of teachers and students. She offers everything you need to plan, teach, and refresh your stations year-round, including

- Step-by-step instructions for launching and maintaining the station;

- Whole group lesson plans, based on key literacy standards, to introduce and support partner work;

- Printable teacher and student tools;

- On-the-spot assessment ideas and troubleshooting tips;

- Lists of grade-level specific materials; and

- Real-classroom photos so you see the possibilities firsthand.

Don't miss the other books in the Simply Stations series!

- Simply Stations: Writing

- Simply Stations: Poetry

- Simply Stations: Drama

- Simply Stations: Word Study

- Simply Stations: Let's Talk

- Simply Stations: Inquiry and Research

To order your copies, visit corwin.com/simplystations

A SAGE Publishing Company

Helping educators make the greatest impact

CORWIN HAS ONE MISSION: to enhance education through intentional professional learning.

We build long-term relationships with our authors, educators, clients, and associations who partner with us to develop and continuously improve the best evidence-based practices that establish and support lifelong learning.